Interior
LANDSCAPES

An American Design Portfolio of Green Environments

First published in the United States of America by
Rockport Publishers, Inc.
33 Commercial Street
Gloucester, Massachusetts 01930-5089
Telephone: (978) 282-9590
Facsimile: (978) 283-2742

Distributed to the book trade and art trade in the United States
by
North Light Books, an imprint of
F & W Publications
1507 Dana Avenue
Cincinnati, Ohio 45207
Telephone: (800) 289-0963

Other Distribution by
Rockport Publishers, Inc.
Gloucester, Massachusetts 01930-5089

ISBN 1-56496-487-6

10 9 8 7 6 5 4 3 2 1

Design: Fahrenheit
Front Cover Images: (top) L. Albee / Longwood Gardens
(bottom) Mine Safety Appliance Company
Back Cover Image: Deere & Company
Printed in China

Interior
LANDSCAPES

An American Design Portfolio of Green Environments

GLOUCESTER MASSACHUSETTS

ROCKPORT
PUBLISHERS

Nelson R. Hammer, ASLA

Introduction by Ronald Wood

To Lora, Daniel, and Alison

ACKNOWLEDGMENTS

The author gets the credit, but—in a work of this nature—the contributors make the book, and this book had many contributors whose assistance was invaluable. I would first like to thank in general all the architects, landscape architects, interior designers, and interior landscape contractors who have been—and continue to be—responsible for the design, construction, and maintenance of plantings indoors, whether or not they contributed to this book. The talent, creativity, and hard work of these people provides untold pleasure to millions who enjoy being in the spaces they have created.

The owners and developers of the projects deserve their fair share of credit for having the foresight to fund interior landscapes, particularly when it may go against the principle of the ubiquitous "bottom line."

The list of specific contributors whose assistance I would like to recognize is quite lengthy, and includes many names that will be unfamiliar to the readers. While this book presents a substantial number of impressive projects, an even larger number of projects were submitted which, for reasons that may seem inexplicable, never made it through the final edit and were not included. The time, effort, and expense expended by these "unseen" contributors was every bit as noteworthy and appreciated as those of the contributors whose efforts are displayed in these pages. I am deeply indebted to all of the following people or firms.

Architectural firms and their staffs:
ADD, The Design Alliance, Sir Norman Foster & Partners, the Hillier Group, HLW International LLP, Lewis & Malm Architecture, Moshe Safdie and Associates, Kevin Roche John Dinkeloo and Associates, Shepley Bulfinch Richardson and Abbott, the Stubbins Associates, Tsoi Kobus and Associates, Voorsanger & Associates, and Wimberly Allison Tong & Goo

Landscape architectural firms and their staffs:
Civil & Civic, CLR Design, EDAW, M. Paul Friedberg & Partners, Grover & Harrison, Joseph Hajnas Associates, Joe Karr & Associates, the Office of Dan Kiley, Landscape Associates, Landscape Images, Mahan Rykiel Associates, the Olin Partnership, Sasaki Associates, Edward Durrell Stone, Jr. & Associates, and Zen Associates

Interior Landscape Contracting firms and their staffs:
Blondie's Treehouse, Diversifolia, John Mini Indoor Landscapes, Landscape Images, Parker Interior Plantscapes, Planterra Tropical Greenhouses, Rentokil Tropical Plant Services, Tropex, and Truscapes

Direct Project Sources:
John Deere and Company, Longwood Gardens, Mine Safety Appliance, Missouri Botanical Gardens

The in- and out-of-house staff of Rockport Publishers, for their help, support, and tolerance of my constant delays while I was trying to make a living during the writing of this book: Jeanine Caunt, Rosalie Grattaroti, Pat O'Maley, Kathy Feerick, Shane Donaldson, and Paul Montie. Their collective efforts have surpassed my wildest expectations for the outcome of this book.

And finally, I would like to thank Ronald Wood, author of the essay "Interior Landscaping, Health, and Well-Being" (included in these pages), for his assistance in writing much of the text, providing his expertise whenever it was requested, and helping to plant the seed in me (pardon the horticultural pun) to write this book.

TABLE OF CONTENTS

[opposite] Rowland Institute
for Science

INTRODUCTION

The use of living plants as an integral element within buildings is a relatively recent phenomenon, made possible by a series of technological advances that provide plants with the necessary environments to sustain themselves indoors. While some of the advances are ancient (the containerization of plants, the inventions of glass and waterproofing), other innovations (air conditioning, electric lighting and heating systems) have been conceived or perfected only since the latter part of the nineteenth century. The first major step towards introducing plants in our homes and offices occurred during the mid-nineteenth century, with the advent of the conservatory in England and Western Europe. This new building type, with its expansive use of vertical and sloped glazing, resulted in buildings designed specifically to grow or display plants; and the importation of exotic tropical and subtropical plants into these new spaces, located in temperate climates, so captivated the public that the "house plant" phenomenon was born. Indoor gardens were here to stay.

Placing a potted fern on a windowsill, however, is a far cry from the use of plants depicted on these pages. In the last three decades the culture, transportation, installation, and maintenance of plants for interior use have been vastly improved and refined, enabling designers and contractors to create awe-inspiring horticultural achievements that can be sustained within environments designed not for plants but for humans. From hotel lobbies to corporate atria to built-in planters in living rooms, plants now transform their surroundings by humanizing the scale of multistory spaces, softening the edges of austere surfaces, and adding vibrant color and texture—all the familiar aesthetic qualities of plant materials. But the role of plants in the interior landscape transcends current fashions; it addresses specific human needs.

Other well-known benefits derived from having plants in our homes and offices are documented in Ronald Wood's essay in this book: the reduction of stress, the increase of productivity, the incentive to remain longer in indoor spaces. His essay also documents more recent and less-known findings—that by metabolizing many indoor air pollutants into plant food, plants can improve the cleanliness of indoor air and make buildings safer and healthier. Not a bad by-product for something valued chiefly for its visual appeal!

Though *Interior Landscapes* focuses on the use of plants in environments intended for people, it also includes some of the diverse examples of contemporary buildings intended primarily for plants, or—as in several examples—for animals other than *Homo Sapiens*. The final chapter illustrates what visitors to the current progeny of the nineteenth-century conservatory might see today.

The projects represented here are a mere fragment of what the interior landscape design and construction disciplines have accomplished in the recent past. It is hoped that these pages will inspire practitioners of these disciplines to find even more innovative ways to use living plants—to create aesthetically pleasing, healthier, more people-friendly interior environments.

Nelson R. Hammer, ASLA

[opposite] Anheuser Busch

Essay

Interior Landscaping:
Health and Well-being

The economic rationalism of the last decade of the twentieth century has caused a critical review of the place of interior landscapes in commercial spaces. If life-cycle costing can't be justified, then landscape is considered only as decoration. Our preoccupation with technology and an international style of functional, environmentally controlled buildings has made it seem that plants and landscaped interiors are out of place. "That people are constantly moving into new environments, unconnected with the natural environment, tends to give the impression that they are enlarging the range of their evolutionary past. This is an illusion because wherever humans go, they can function only to the extent that they maintain a micro environment that is similar to the one from which they evolved."[1]

[1]Yeang K., (1995), Designing With Nature , The Ecological Basis for Architectural Design, McGraw Hill New York.

Nature and the modern indoor environment

The term "building ecology" has been used to describe a comprehensive systems approach to understanding interactions between building environments and their occupants. People react to indoor environments in markedly different ways. Complex modern building environments produce reactions of a psychological (perceptual) and physiological (biological) nature, sometimes affecting people in visceral ways. The reasons why one environment is better than another are complex; besides the physical environment itself there are all the psychosocial factors that pertain to it, especially in the workplace. Traditionally this has been the field of the management analyst; it is becoming clear, however, that the physical and psychological work environments are not separate entities but rather parts of a single integrated experience.

Focusing on the benefits of plants for healthy and comfortable indoor environments

In recent years, researchers from several disciplines, including clinical psychology, environmental psychology, sociology, and behavioral medicine, have been investigating the benefits of contacts with plants. People derive benefits from plants in a wide range of situa-

[opposite] LOM Technologies, Inc.

tions, through active involvement such as gardening or more passively, perhaps, by looking at plants through a window. People interact with the total indoor environment, which either supports and satisfies them in their tasks or hinders and frustrates. It is estimated that Americans spend ninety percent of their time inside buildings, seven percent in cars, and only three percent outdoors. The office is where many of us spend most of our waking hours and should thus be seen as a second home; we should be able to personalize it the same way we adjust lighting, ventilation, or layout in the place we live. We need a sense of connection with events beyond our desk, a connectedness with other workers, the organization, and the outside world. Isolation can be negative, a form of sensory deprivation. The landscaped atrium, combining daylight with nature, provides a good antidote to the confinement of cube or office. The natural setting or interior plantscaping have been found to provide visual relief and relaxation for workers spending long periods at a desk, visual display unit, or drawing board.

Stress-reducing effects of plants

Although certain kinds of short-term stress can improve human performance and cognitive functioning, the long-term effects of stress are deleterious. Research focused on the indoor environment shows that natural settings with vegetation can help people cope with stress and deal more effectively with workplace requirements.

Plants and indoor air

People occupy a building in the belief that their working environment is safe. A healthy building is one that does not adversely affect the health of its occupants or the larger environment. A building's air quality is thus a major indoor environmental issue.

The ability of plants to absorb chemicals from the environment and biodegrade them has been demonstrated in many studies. Former NASA scientist Dr. Bill Wolverton has shown that common varieties of interior foliage plants can reduce the concentrations of various trace organic chemicals such as formaldehyde, benzene, and trichloroethane injected into sealed test chambers. More recent work at the University of Technology, Sydney, has confirmed these findings and shown that potted indoor plants can also remove volatile organic compounds (VOCs) from the atmosphere. Kentia Palm in particular can remove several times the occupational levels of benzene and hexane, and its ability to do so is increased by exposure to the VOCs concerned. Plants, in other words, can reduce indoor air pollution and may function as a metabolic sink for many trace contaminants.

An outstanding feature of plant response to many synthetic air pollutants is a variable adjustment to acute or constant exposure. Airborne chemicals are absorbed by leaves and broken down by plant respiration into carbon dioxide and water, normal products that building occupants also exhale. Healthy plants in the office may be the equivalent of canaries in the coal mine.

The Economics of good indoor air quality

While indoor air quality (IAQ) can influence the work environment, other ingredients affect the well-being, comfort, and tolerance of building occupants—lighting, noise, vibration, and overcrowding; ergonomics and interior design; company organization and culture; job satisfaction, security, health, and family-related problems. Though a building's operating costs are tangible, productivity gains or losses are less so. A small decrease in productivity can be costly; a one-percent productivity loss is roughly four times the cost of heating and cooling the building.

Employee dissatisfaction is often directed towards air-conditioning systems, perceived lack of "air" or variations in temperature—comfort factors that can be tested and usually corrected. Working in a "sick" building will negatively affect productivity. How productive are workers when more than twenty percent complain about their work environment? Has absenteeism increased? Are workers spending more time away from their offices? Are people working effectively?

Improving the work environment requires a multidisciplinary approach, one that involves the building owner, architect, systems engineer, manager, operator, and tenants. Implicit in the provision of good IAQ is the assumption that the building and its systems are properly designed and performing as intended.

Psychological well-being

A growing interest in human interaction with "nature" has recently directed research toward the benefits of people/plant relationships in the indoor environment. Increasingly, this research has focused on aesthetics.

If plant-filled settings elicit aesthetic responses, individuals might be expected to express pleasure in measurable ways. Not surprisingly, studies show that people usually prefer nature scenes dominated by vegetation to urban scenes lacking it. While the aesthetic response is emotionally important, it is only one of the broad range of feelings (e.g. interest, anger, sadness, fear) central to issues of stress and restoration.

Health-related benefits

Recent technical advances have furthered research on the beneficial influences of contact with plants. Electronics miniaturization and computers can now record physiological indicators such as blood pressure, heart rate, muscle contraction, and electrical activity of the brain. Eye-tracking equipment can measure the actual attention given to plants and vegetation. These advances enable researchers to apply physiological and health-related procedures in a broad range of real-world situations, such as offices, workplaces, and health-care facilities.

Restorative or stress-reducing responses may be seen as adaptive strategies in human evolution, balancing negatively toned affects such as fear and aggression and reducing deleterious mobilization of the sympathetic nervous system (as in the case of high blood pressure). Such responses engage the parasympathetic nervous system associated with the maintenance or recharging of energy. Positive emotional states elicited by natural settings may significantly increase people's scores on creativity tests and high-order functioning.

Physiological evidence of benefits of plants

Besides psychological effects, stress and restoration have important physiological dimensions, involving responses and activity level in bodily systems such as the cardiovascular. Data obtained by recording physiological responses are widely recognized as indicators of stress and restoration. Physiological methods may also identify influences on well-being outside an individual's conscious awareness.

In a major study at the University of Technology, Sydney, brain electrical activity in unstressed individuals viewing either a whiteboard, an abstract painting, or an indoor foliage plant showed an increase of alpha wave activity in subjects viewing the plant. Apart from indicating that the whiteboard/abstract painting had different effects on electrocortical activity, the alpha wave results strongly suggest that the foliage plant was more effective in eliciting a wakeful, relaxed state. In similar studies elsewhere, it has been found that vegetation settings sustain attention and interest at higher levels than do urban scenes, and produce more positively toned emotional states. This higher alpha wave activity is located in the brain's right hemisphere, suggesting a creative, as well as a wakeful, relaxed state. Other kinds of physiological tests have shown that visitors to botanical gardens experience an actual decrease in systolic blood pressure.

Such results suggest that people may not need to be consciously aware of plants in their indoor environments to benefit from their presence. Scientific approaches based on mere verbal ratings or evaluations of plant-filled settings may not reveal the full effects of plants on well-being.

Plants: nature's humidifiers

The control of relative humidity is important for thermal comfort and may introduce difficulties in the maintenance of the desired range, particularly during winter. Indoor plants can contribute to increased interior humidity by adding moisture to the air through natural transpiration through their leaves. The amount of moisture plants may contribute is influenced by many interrelated factors, such as plant species, temperature, light levels, and the moisture content of the growing media. Natural variability in the rate of transpiration influenced by these factors leads to a measure of self-control, minimizing the likelihood of excessive amounts of moisture being added to the indoor environment. Plants added to an office building with a forced-air system may significantly increase the relative humidity.

Contemporary theories

Among the theories that attempt to explain the benefits of passive contact with plants is the "psychoevolutionary" perspective, which holds that quick-onset affective or emotional reactions—not cognitive responses—constitute the first level of response to nature, and underly all subsequent thoughts, memory, meaning, and behavior with respect to environments. This position is consistent with a large body of contemporary research on emotions and cognition, and with recent advances in neurophysiology.

Conclusion

Natural settings provided the context of everyday experience throughout human evolution. The understanding of positive human response to nature represents a major new direction for scientific research, one that can help us learn more about ourselves and the benefits we derive from natural environments. By contributing solid evidence of the importance of plants for human well-being, research in health psychology, clinical psychology, and behavioral medicine will help decision makers give higher priority to plants in the indoor environment. Designing with living plants makes interior spaces not only look good but good for our health as well.

Ronald Wood

Commercial

Copley Place:

Looking down from the upper mall level, a single line of red Azaleas (*Rhododendron* spp.) makes its way through the dense plantings of the large plant bed.

(Below) Several days after opening, the ground cover in the large plant bed is already a uniform carpet of solid green and the uplights illuminate the foliage of the three 25-foot (7.6- meter) trees.

Store owners and facility managers are well aware of the benefits of creating pleasant, enjoyable atmospheres that encourage shoppers to spend time in their retail environments.

Creative interior landscapes transport customers from the everyday world outside into totally different environments that make them feel good and ensure their return. Plant-oriented design changes can accommodate changing merchandise displays, direct traffic flow through the mall, and help attract return visits from shoppers. The projects illustrated highlight the success of these important design considerations for people and plants in offices and shopping malls.

Parkway North Center
DEERFIELD, ILLINOIS

Parkway North is a 1-million square-foot (92,900-square-meter) office development in Deerfield, Illinois. A five-story atrium occupies one-third of the total building space. Forty large-specimen Weeping Fig trees *(Ficus benjamina)* and Black Olive *(Bucida buceras)* trees were brought in by crane and planted prior to the installation of the curtain-wall glazing. 170 tons (154,221 kilograms) of natural boulders were skillfully positioned to protect delicate moss colonies in several atrium locations. Lush underplanting, elaborate flower displays, stone outcroppings, flagstone paving, and a bubbling stream combine to make a luxuriant garden.

1.

2.

3.

1. The interplay of natural light through the tree canopies creates dramatic shadow patterns on the understory plantings and pavements below. The mood of the garden changes as the sun travels overhead.

2. This vibrant display of red Poinsettias *(Euphorbia pulcherrima)* warms the atrium with holiday color and uplifts the spirit of its visitors.

3. A bluestone walkway winds through the atrium beneath the canopies of Black Olive *(Bucida buceras)* and Weeping Fig *(Ficus benjamina)* trees.

1.

2.

3.

1. Masses of pink flowering Impatiens *(Impatiens* spp.*)* are just a part of the spring flower selection.

2. The garden is a place where employees can retreat from the work environment for a few moments of restorative conversation.

3. An assortment of textures intrigues the eye. The handsome, broad leaves of Elephant's Ear *(Alocasia* spp.*)* share planting space with the soft, delicate fronds of a Boston Fern *(Nephrolepis exaltata 'Bostoniensis').*

2.

1. At midday, the atrium serves as a park-like café with food service available at the south end of the garden.

2. Scheduling and coordination among trades played a critical role in the installation process.

3. A Black Olive tree *(Bucida buceras)* in the background is silhouetted as the afternoon sun drenches the atrium.

3.

Matt Bird, Diversifolia, Inc.
St. Louis, Missouri

744 Office Parkway Office Building
ST. LOUIS, MISSOURI

Before being renovated, the interior of this office building was outdated; the extensive atrium beds were overgrown and they lacked any sense of design clarity. After the architects redesigned the lobbies, the beds were reconfigured using similar species in the various planters to provide simplicity and continuity. With a relatively limited budget, large material was not a design option. The selected feature plants Thread Palms *(Washingtonia robusta)* were only 7 to 8 feet (2.1 to 2.4 meters) in height, but it was felt the bold texture and size of their fronds would provide a full, uniform appearance. To draw attention to the underplantings, Chinese Fan Palms *(Livistona chinensis)* were chosen to mimic the appearance of the taller specimens. The ground covers used were Jade Pothos *(Epipremnum aureum 'Tropic Green')* and Starlight Peace Lilies *(Spathiphyllum 'Starlight')*.

Seasonals bloomers and Bromeliads bring fresh, new highlights to the office on a regular basis.

1.

2.

1. To create a sense of rhythm and continuity, the large, coarse-textured foliage of Thread Palms *(Washingtonia robusta)* was used throughout the space, while the white blooming Starlight Peace Lily *(Spathiphyllum 'Starlight')* adds contrast.

2. and 3. Chinese Fan Palm *(Livistona chinensis)* leaves repeat the bold look provided by the Thread Palms, providing this texture at different heights for the viewer. The thick ground cover of Jade Pothos *(Epipremnum aureum 'Tropic Green')* provides a dense mass of green, and seasonals give a splash of color to the planters.

3.

Menlo Park Mall

MENLO PARK, NEW JERSEY

Menlo Park is an upscale suburban shopping mall with two major department stores and 170 specialty stores. Feature plantings include sixteen 18- to 20-foot (5.5 to 6.1-meter) Weeping Podocarpus *(Podocarpus gracilior)*, two 16-foot (4.9-meter) Adonidia Palms *(Veitcha Merillii)*, three 12-foot (3.7-meter) Black Olive trees *(Bucida buceras)*, fifteen English Ivy *(Hedera Helix)* topiaries 3 to 14 feet (.9 to 4.3 meters) tall, and a grove of 12- to 14-foot (3.7- to 4.3-meter) Indian Laurel Fig trees *(Ficus nitida)*. Nearly 300 Bromeliad and seasonal flowers are rotated regularly.

1.

2.

1. The Fountain Court with its glass elevator and clock tower. 16-foot (5.5-meter) Adonidia Palms *(Veitchia Merrillii)* flank the tower. Flowers are changed regularly.

2. Overall view of the main avenue of the mall, showing several trees with under-plantings as well as balcony plantings.

3. The Food Court features a grove of 20-foot (6.1-meter) Weeping Fig trees *(Ficus benjamina)* along with topiary English Ivy and colorful sculpture.

3.

Mayfair Mall
WAUWATOSA, WISCONSIN

A twenty-five-year-old shopping mall in a north-west suburb of Milwaukee required a facelift to compete with more modern malls in the area. The central interior open space, with an ice-skating rink as its focal feature, was dated and in declining condition.

To add vitality and excitement, the central space was extended to nearly twice its height and enclosed in glass. Spacious pedestrian fingers were widened and connected to other brightly lit atria nodes. Groups of large movable planters enhance the shop-lined fingers, but large, unique, in-ground tree installations dominate the central space and the atria.

1.

2.

3.

1. At the center garden, four grids—consisting of four planting pockets each—frame an ever-changing multiple-activity space that shoppers pass through or view from upper levels.

2. A grid of specially designed planters with 20-foot (6.1-meter) high multistem Weeping Fig trees *(Ficus benjamina)* identify the crossing of two pedestrian corridors. Algerian Ivy *(Hedera canariensis)* drapes over the planter edges. In the distance, trees of another species mark a node.

3. Sunlight streaming in from the overhead skylight is absorbed by the golden stems of the delicately leafed Native Bamboo trees *(Bambusa vulgaris aereo-variegatus)*. Ever-changing shadows from the towering trees reflect on the walking surface where shoppers pass.

1.

1. The golden stems of copses of 40-foot (12.2-meter) Native Bamboo trees *(Bambusa vulgaris aereo-variegatus)*, arranged in a grid of four pockets, provide vertical scale in the high, open central atrium.

2. The bright golden and internodal green-striped stems of the Native Bamboo trees *(Bambusa vulgaris aereo-variegatus)* emerge from dense beds of Fortnight Lily *(Moraea iridoides)* at each 6-foot by 6-foot (1.8-meter by 1.8-meter) planting pocket.

2.

M. Paul Friedberg & Partners
New York, New York

Bamboo *(Phyllostachys aurea)* installed in the 28 Queen's Road, Central, Hong Kong

The importation of Bamboo *(Phyllostachys aurea)* from the United States to a part of the world in which Bamboo is native made this project highly unusual. Investigations indicated that Bamboo species more readily available to the site were not suitable for indoor use and it was decided to provide the Bamboo from a U.S. source. To import it through Hong Kong customs, the product had to shipped without any soil whatsoever. It was air-freighted in custom-made crates supplied with specially created water-misting systems to prevent the roots from drying. In Hong Kong, the planting medium had to be created from locally available materials: pulverized coconut husks were a main component. Custom-designed containers made from steel pipes and soil separator were quite heavy due to excessive rains. On completion, the Bamboo were the largest indoor plants in Hong Kong.

1. The casual viewer of this dense grove of Bamboo *(Phyllostachys Aurea)* would never realize the logistical maze through which it travelled to arrive in a downtown Hong Kong office building

2. The interior landscape contractor found the Bamboo *(Phyllostachys aurea)* in Florida and shipped it to Hong Kong in special wooden crates with a self-contained misting system.

3. Unloading a crate of Bamboo *(Phyllostachys aurea)* in a special Hong Kong nursery subcontracted by the interior landscape contractor, to be potted up and grown for the installation at the job site.

1.

4.

2.

3.

1. Viewed from the upper mall level, the 60-foot (18.3-meter) granite, marble, and travertine water sculpture is quite dramatic.

2. The base of the waterfall becomes the source of a marble-edged stream, the banks of which are heavily planted with ground covers and massed shrubs.

3. An above-grade wedding cake planter is decked out in holiday flowers and tivoli lights.

4. Trailing runners of Needle-point Ivy *(Hedera Helix 'Needlepoint')* are trained to cascade over the marble streambed edge.

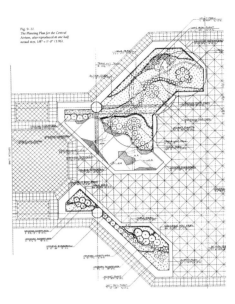

Fig. 9–11.
The Planting Plan for the Central
Atrium, also reproduced at one half
actual size. 1/8" = 1'-0" (1:96).

1.

2.

3.

1. A partial planting plan of the Central Atrium space shows the use of massed ground covers, understory plantings, an irregular line of seasonal plants, and the three trees.

2. Stepped plantings follow the escalators up to the second level of the mall.

3. A scene reminiscent of the Marine flag raising on Iwo Jima is repeated whenever large trees are installed indoors without the benefit of mechanized equipment.

4. A professional rendering of the Central Atrium prepared during schematic design bears striking resemblance to the completed mall. Only the water feature, which was redesigned after the rendering was prepared, appears to depart from the finished product. (Rendering by Howard Associates.)

5. A section through the large plant bed illustrates how the soil level must be raised to accommodate the root ball of one of the large trees. Lightweight fill is used between the bottom of the planter and the planting medium to reduce weight and restrain planting medium costs.

4.

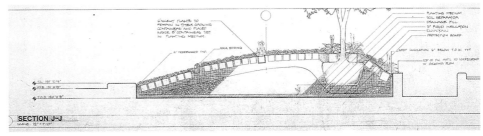

5.

Lois S. Harrison, Grover & Harrison, P.C.
Birmingham, Alabama

Lenox Square Expansion and Renovation
ATLANTA, GEORGIA

For two generations, shoppers have come to Lenox Square from all over the southeast. With the growing attraction of Atlanta as a world-market center and site of the 1996 Olympics, the mall underwent extensive architectural expansion and renovation to create a European retail experience.

The greatest challenge was the execution, coordination, and installation of fifty topiary specimens from 6 to 12 feet (1.8 to 3.7 meters) in height. The development of the 12-foot (3.7-meter) avian topiaries from California required the most attention. The only live foliage was used on the first section of topiaries, within close reach and visual inspection of shoppers. The remaining specimens required much research to provide the most realistic artificial foliage on the market.

1.

2.

3.

4.

1. Two large Black Olive trees *(Bucida buceras)* underplanted with ground cover are placed in planters surrounded by seating.

2. For the interior landscape, different types of plants and topiaries helped distinguish the European-style town squares in front of the department stores from the gallery spaces between.

3. Palms and fig trees add color and texture to the mall.

4. Throughout the mall, seventeenth-century European 12-foot (3.7-meter) topiary forms were translated into the twenty-first century to announce access points to the new second-floor shops and to provide living sculpture.

Nelson Hammer, Hammer Design
Boston, Massachusetts

Maine Mall Renovation
SOUTH PORTLAND, MAINE

The State of Maine's largest regional mall was originally constructed with two anchor department stores in 1971 and expanded with three more department-store anchors in 1982. The architect was commissioned in 1992 by the mall's owner-managers to design a complete renovation that would redefine the older shopping center into Maine's premiere shopping destination. A key to the renovation was an increase in natural lighting, using expanded areas of clear and fritted glazing in larger skylights, helping to create a more enticing environment for plants.

The design solution highlights three major spaces—the Food Court, the Center Court, and the Garden Court, each of which reflects an aspect of Maine's history and culture.

The new Food Court seats five hundred and features strong references to Maine's history in design motifs that recall the traditional agriculture fair with environmental graphics, signage, and lighting expressing this spirit. The new Center Court reduces the clutter and brings in more natural light. The executed design contains elements of the classic Maine meeting

1.

"ER THAN THE SOUL IS HIGH."   "LIVES OF GREAT MEN

2.

3.

FRUIT AND VEGETABLE SALADS
FRESH FROM THE GARDEN

4.

1. The plant-filled Garden Court reflects Maine's natural beauty. Centered above a handmade mosaic floor inspired by gardens found in Northeast Harbor is a neon-lighted sun.

2. The Center Court contains elements of the classic Maine meeting house. To provide for a variety of promotional events, all furniture and plantings can be easily moved and rearranged.

3. The new Food Court edges are defined by a series of low ceramic planters with Hawaiian Schefflera (Schefflera arboricola).

4. The Center Court features a large new skylight, Black Olive trees (Bucida buceras) in black ceramic planters, and Maria Chinese Evergreen trees (Aglaonema 'Maria') in custom-designed wood planters on casters.

house and highlights the voices of Maine's social and literary leaders. To provide for a variety of promotional events, furniture and plantings in custom-designed wood planters on casters are easily moved. The aptly named Garden Court is filled with trees and ground covers, reflecting Maine's natural beauty. Centered above is a copper-leafed and neon-lighted sun, which is suspended below a large pyramidal skylight.

HLW International LLP
New York, New York

Located on New York City's prestigious Park Avenue, the Chem Court garden represents a gift of greenery to the people of New York from Chemical Bank. Chemical Bank had provided for 12,500 square feet (1,080 square meters) of space to be filled with trees, underplantings, and terraced pools. The entire interior garden involved the creative use of foliage plants. Many were highly unusual while others were breathtaking examples of more common varieties: ninety-one specimens of Common Bamboo *(Bambusa vulgaris)* ranging in height from 12 feet (3.7 meters) to 36 feet (11 meters), three Mexican Fig tree *(Ficus mexicana)*, six 8-foot (2.4-meter) to 14-foot (4.3-meter) Black Olive trees *(Bucida buceras)*, which completely defoliated three weeks after installation—but as is their nature, came back strong!—six Autograph trees *(Clusia rosea)* ranging in size from 5 feet (1.5 meters) to 12 feet (3.7 meters), a 95-gallon (365-liter) Madagascar Dragon tree *(Dracaena marginata)*, a 16-foot (4.9-meter) Lance Dracaena *(Dracaena reflexa)*, twelve 16-foot (4.9-meter) to 18-foot (5.5-meter) Weeping Fig trees *(Ficus benjamina)*, two Umbrella trees *(Schefflera actinophylla)* ranging from

1.

1. A planter bed is shown with a large variety of species, plus hanging plants cascading down from the upper floors.

[opposite] A view of the pyramidal truss at the entrance covered with cascading vines.

3.

22 feet (6.7 meters) to 35 feet (10.7 meters), and four Ponytail Palms *(Beaucarnea recurvata)* between 8 feet (2.4 meters) and 15 feet (4.6 meters) in height. A great deal of effort went into the landscape design of Chem Court, with consideration cooperation from growers in Florida to meet the specific size and shape of design requirements. The design intent was to create a horticultural environment not limited to familiar plant varieties. The attractive glass structure enclosing the garden allows the plantings to be viewed not only from within but from the outside as well.

[opposite] Pothos *(Epipremnum aureum)* and other hanging vines illustrate how comprehensively architecture and interior landscaping interreact at Chem Court.

3. A row of matched Black Olive trees *(Bucida buceras)* makes a bold textural statement in the foreground, with another Black Olive specimen of different character behind it.

Wintergarden, Battery Park City
NEW YORK, NEW YORK

"A new town in town" was built on a landfill site in lower Manhattan by the State of New York, in concert with the City of New York. This urban complex includes the World Financial Center at Battery Park City, 7 million square feet (630,000 square meters) of office space, and New York City's first waterfront plaza. The location on New York's Hudson River is dramatic—the project faces the harbor with a distant view of the Statue of Liberty.

A keystone of the project is the Wintergarden, an enclosed urban space filled with sixteen Thread Palms *(Washingtonia robusta)*. In order to acclimatize the palms, the interior landscape contractor custom-built the largest shade house in the United States (at the time) in the California desert, near where the palms were located, and grew them there for two years. When the building was ready for the installation, the trees were transported by truck from California to New York, stopping approximately every 200 miles (320 kilometers) to water the root balls and wet the foliage.

For supplemental plant-growth lighting, special high-intensity discharge lights were provided to raise light intensities to an acceptable level. A drip irrigation system was installed to water the trees, which require irrigation twice per week.

1.

2.

3.

4.

1., 2., 3. Various views of the palms in place at the World Financial Center, Battery Park City.

4. The country's largest (at the time) shade house was custom built in the desert to acclimatize the sixteen palms that will go into the Wintergarden.

590 Madison Avenue
NEW YORK, NEW YORK

With nearly three hundred Bamboo Trees *(Phyllostachys nigra 'Henon')* standing 30 feet (9.1 meters) to 45 feet (13.7 meters) tall, the Garden Plaza (in the building that was formerly IBM's corporate headquarters in Manhattan) has the charm of a living green cathedral. There are twenty-five Bamboo culms in each of eleven pits. To people walking through or pausing at tables and chairs in the Garden Plaza, the towering Bamboo trees create an atmosphere of serenity, almost majesty. However, Bamboo—a member of the grass family that flourishes predominantly in tropical climates—was still a new and experimental species for building interiors at the time of the initial installation. To make an outstanding impression in as architecturally striking a setting as the 590 Madison Avenue, Garden Plaza became a considerable horticultural challenge, requiring the precise monitoring of all environmental conditions.

1.

1. Sunlight filtering through the Bamboo foliage creates a dappled effect on the granite floor of the Garden Plaza.

2. The towering Bamboo extends 30 feet (9.1 meters) to 45 feet (13.7 meters) over the atrium floor, filling the soaring space.

3. Graceful culms of Bamboo— twenty-five plants in each of the eleven pits—create a living green cathedral during the holidays.

2.

3.

River Oaks Mall

CALUMET CITY, ILLINOIS

River Oaks Center opened in 1966 as an open-air retail center. In early 1993, the owner announced plans to enclose, renovate, and expand the center to a total build-out of 1.2 million square feet. The design intent was to maintain the unique open-air atmosphere within a totally enclosed facility, using Weeping Fig trees *(Ficus benjamina)* to provide the shade tree type plant form. Raised planted areas were planted with Chinese Evergreen *(Agloanema spp.)*, Peace Lily *(Spathiphyllum spp.)*, Hawaiian Schefflera *(Schefflera arboricola)*, and Pothos *(Epipremnum aureum)* to provide massed green areas with a profile to allow visability of storefronts and signage. Architectural planting bowls were incorporated near seating areas and planted with annuals to provide seasonal color.

1.

3.

2.

1. Bright flowering seasonals add the impact of color. They are used in custom fabricated bowls mounted to sloping wood surfaces throughout concourse seating areas.

2. A Weeping Fig tree (*Ficus benjamina*) provides a canopy for Food Court patrons, creating a park type setting.

3. Water cascades down a series of steps bordered by colorful blooming plants. Camille Dumb Cane (*Dieffenbachia 'Camille'*) is used to soften the confluence of the waterfall and the reflecting pool.

Corporate

The corporate headquarters facility offers two distinct advantages over the hotel atrium or shopping mall in its ability to display interior plants: heightened security and reduced pedestrian traffic. Heavy pedestrian use in malls or hotels forces the interior landscape designer to use species tolerant of physical abuse and to restrict plant placement wherever possible so as not to endanger delicate foliage.

Corporate headquarters rarely suffer these limitations, displaying a more diverse palette of species and a more direct interrelation between plants and people. With lower volumes of people passing through and better control over those who do, incidental damage and vandalism are greatly reduced. Interior gardens (in the literal, visual sense) become possible, offering employees a more natural and soothing setting in the midst of an otherwise typical workplace.

Corporate interior landscapes can also enjoy more specific thematic elements than other building types; while mall and hotel landscapes are often fairly generic in concept, the corporate atrium may instill a company's philosophy into the interior design, furnishings, art work, and plantings. Unusual species, specimens of extraordinary size, and extravagant floral displays are among the various elements that distinguish the corporate interior landscape. These elements are made possible or enhanced by the higher level of maintenance afforded by corporations to the premier spaces in their buildings.

Deere & Company Corporate Headquarters: This is the third-floor view looking south. The black-bricked second-floor walkway cuts across the center of the atrium, affording expansive views in all directions. Two gambrel skylights bathing the atrium in daylight actually allow only twenty percent light transmission.

As an international supplier of lawn- and garden-maintenance equipment, Deere & Company of Moline, Illinois sets the tone for the quality of its product line with a vast but impeccably maintained atrium interior landscape in its West Atrium headquarters, built in 1978. Although the landscape design is pure and elegant, the health of the plantings—the neatly trimmed ground covers, the gloss of foliage, and the pruning of larger specimens—deserves as much credit as the design itself for the overall visual effect.

Deere & Company Headquarters
MOLINE, ILLINOIS

The West Office Building is the most recent of three structures, nestled between two lakes in the Rock River Valley near Moline, Illinois, which house the corporate headquarters of Deere & Company, a manufacturer of farm equipment. Deere West features a two-and-a-half story skylit atrium filled with 11,000 square feet (1,021 square meters) of heavily landscaped natural terrain. Completed years ago, the atrium remains the focal point of Deere's administrative complex.

The cafeteria opens out onto the garden at ground level, and offices on the second and third floors overlook the landscape without interference from interior window partitions. Despite a light transmittance through the skylight glazing of only twenty percent, the control of plant growth has been a significant maintenance responsibility, which is handled by Deere staff in-house. Plant substitutions and rotations are supplied entirely by four greenhouses located on the Deere & Company campus.

1.

1. The atrium is no less impressive at night. Lights are for general illumination and are not specifically intended to assist in plant growth. While artificially located, the boulders are carefully sited and covered with ground cover plants to further enhance their natural effect on the landscape.

2. First-floor view looking north towards the cafeteria. The walkway consists of large slabs of granite laid in a diagonal pattern to direct traffic flow while reinforcing the atrium's geometry. Paver joints are in-filled with ground cover to enhance the garden effect.

3. The stark contrast between the garden and the built environment around is evident in this view looking toward an employee lounge.

4. Looking north from the south end of the atrium, the drop in topography from south to north is evident as natural stone formations and granite stairs help create the change in grade.

2.

3.

4.

Joseph Hajnas & Elizabeth R. Manuck, Joseph Hajnas Associates, Inc.
Pittsburgh, Pennsylvania

Mine Safety Appliance Company
PITTSBURGH, PENNSYLVANIA

The headquarters of Mine Safety Appliances Company is located in suburban Pittsburgh on an 11-acre (4.5-hectare) site. Inside the chrome-and-glass building is a rectangular atrium measuring 60 feet by 208 feet (18.3 meters by 63.4 meters), topped with a barrel-vaulted, tinted-glass skylight that runs the length of the atrium and provides the plantings below with copious amounts of natural light. The walkthrough garden is accessible on the first floor and easily visible from floors two and three. A diagonal walkway on the second floor completes the atrium design while allowing employees access to the space.

Original soils on the atrium floor were amended and top-dressed with 12 inches (31 cm) of specially formulated planting medium. The broad range of tropical plants thrive in the atrium.

Granite provides color and texture for the walk pavers and steps. Water flows continuously to pools and then recirculates through polished, rectangular granite channels.

1.

2.

3.

1. Looking down from the third floor on the second-floor bridge spanning the atrium.

2. Sunset is met with the warmth of bright lights at the building's main entrance.

3. This oblique angle high-lights the textural and color changes in the two types of granite: the dark polished water-feature edge and the lighter, thermal-finished paving stones.

1. Peace Lilies *(Spathiphyllum spp.)* flourish in the growing medium, providing abundant white spathes reminiscent of Calla Lilies *(Zantedeschia aethiopica)*.

2. Granite steps connect the two sides of the atrium with a tiny footbridge crossing the linear water feature.

3. As seen from the third floor, the elongated water feature spills into a pool partially shown in the foreground.

4. The southern wall of the headquarters facility includes steps, walks, and viewing platforms overlooking the pond.

1.

2.

3.

4.

Joe Karr & Associates
Chicago, Illinois

International Mineral and Chemical Corporation
NORTHBROOK, ILLINOIS

Sitting softly in a rolling landscape, International Mineral and Chemical's corporate world headquarters rests deep in an 11-acre (4.5-hectare) wooded site in a park-like setting. Two large courtyards within the building were originally planned to be open to the sky, but subsequent energy evaluations and climate-related utilization studies established the advantage of enclosing them. With this decision, their year-round visibility was greatly enhanced and their potential use expanded as overflow space for conferences and other organizational functions.

The courtyards, though spatially identical, have been treated quite differently. One is lushly planted, while the other is surfaced with brick pavers on which large moveable planters can be rearranged to conform to functions. The contrast is striking.

1.

2.

1. A potted Striped Dracaena *(Dracaena deremensis 'Warnecki')* is in the foreground, while a row of Silver Queen Chinese Evergreen *(Aglaonema 'Silver Queen')* and an edging of English Ivy *(Hedera Helix)* form a border to the garden proper.

2. Multi-stemmed Weeping Fig trees *(Ficus benjamina)*, Peace Lilies *(Spathiphyllum spp.)* and Hawaiian Schefflera *(Schefflera arboricola)* rise from the English Ivy *(Hedera Helix)* ground cover bed to create the appearance of a temperate climate with tropical plants.

3. The center of the courtyard garden is a low circular ground-cover bed defined by a concentric ring of changing floral plants and an enclosing brick path. Weeping Fig trees *(Ficus benjamina)* echo the simple rhythm while Fatsia shrubs *(Fatsia japonica)* provide contrasting interest.

3.

Bradford Exchange
NILES, ILLINOIS

The Bradford Exchange is the world's largest trading center in collectors' plates. Employing more than 200 office personnel, it is head-quartered in a former 200-foot by 200-foot (61-meter by 61-meter) one-story Sears department store. The spacious openness of the building with a 40-foot by 40-foot (12.2-meter by 12.2-meter) column grid was very suitable for rede-velopment as an open-plan office interior. The center portion of the interior, 30 feet (9.1 meters) long by 100 feet (30.5 meters) wide, was developed as a garden, with three lineally aligned, recessed garden pockets.

The design intent was to allow the garden to be the central focus of the offices, not only as one approaches and sees it through glass from outside the building, but also as one enters the reception area and circu-lates through the garden and across the offices. For office personnel it also functions as a series of semi-isolated conference spaces and a dining area. The subtle sound of the running brook permeates the entire office area.

1.

2.

3.

1. The innermost garden pocket, recessed two feet, contains the dining area with seating around the pool and water source for the continuously running brook.

2. The central garden pocket is sunk 2 feet (0.6 meters) below surrounding walkways. Clay soil excavated from the garden comprises the planted berm outside the reception entrance for screening the parking lot.

3. A wooden seat island accessible by a light wooden bridge nestles in the pool recessed in the reception garden pocket. The plate museum appears in the background.

1.

1. The servery of the lunchtime French restaurant/lounge is tucked under a mezzanine garden over-look accessible from a spiral metal staircase hidden by Weeping Fig trees *(Ficus benjamina)*.

2. Rippling softly over stones, the brook meanders under the fronds of Boston Ferns *(Nephrolepis exal-tata 'Bostoniensis')* and past Pit-tosporum shrubs *(Pittosporum tobira)*, Kangaroo Vine *(Cissus antarctica)*, and Creeping Fig ground cover *(Ficus pumila)* draped over lannon-stone outcroppings.

3. Recirculating through the entire length of the garden and connect-ing the three garden pockets by passing under minibridges and crosswalks, the brook provides the gentle sound of moving water.

2.

3.

The Stubbins Associates
Cambridge, Massachusetts

Zen Associates
Sudbury, Massachusetts

Sited along the Charles River in Cambridge, Massachusetts, The Rowland Institute for Science is a private, nonprofit research institute oriented to pure science. The building was specifically designed to encourage intellectual exchange and interaction among scientists of all disciplines.

The focal point of the Institute's second level is a two-story skylighted atrium with plantings reminiscent of New England woods and meadows. Bluestone paths wind between knolls covered with moss and ground covers. Seating in and around the landscaped space provides quiet gathering areas for conversation. A central horseshoe stair connects the atrium level, the third-floor mezzanine, and the greenhouse laboratory.

Avoiding a typical arrangement of commonly used tropical plants, the atrium is an experimental garden in keeping with the Institute's precepts. Supplemental metal-halide lights provide a minimum of 200 foot-candles fourteen hours a day to maintain some of the more exotic specimens. Mexican Rosarite red beach stones lie along the edges of the atrium and below the upper-level walkways,

1.

where there was insufficient light for plant growth. The garden inspires meditative strolling and conversation and provides a welcome respite for researchers and scientists.

1. To create the feeling of a New England countryside, the meadow areas of the garden consist of a variety of ground covers, including English Baby Tears *(Nertera granadensis)*, Baby's Tears *(Soleirolia Soleirolii)*, and Mondo Grass *(Ophiopogon japonicus)*.

2. Studies completed while the garden was in design indicated that 200 foot-candles of light, fourteen hours a day, would be required to maintain the plant materials proposed for the space. Metal-halide fixtures supplement the atrium's natural light to assure proper light levels.

3. The flagstone walk is infilled with Haircap Moss *(Polytrichum* spp.*)*, which cleanly borders the Baby's Tears *(Soleirolia Soleirolii)* ground cover.

[overleaf] Delicate Holly Fern *(Cyrtomium falcatum)*, Button Fern *(Pellaea rotundifolia)* and Bromeliads contrast with the coarse leaves of Bear's Paw Ferns *(Aglaomorpha Meyeniana)* and Japanese Pittosporum *(Pittosporum tobira)* to provide a variety of textures.

2.

3.

1.

1. The meadow lines one side of the atrium, while the woods—composed of taller plant materials, including Bamboo *(Bambusa* spp.*)*, Black Olive *(Bucida buceras)*, and Southern Yew *(Podocarpus macrophyllus 'Maki')*—line the other.

2. While all very low elements, the juxtaposition of Baby's Tears *(Soleirolia Soleirolii)*, moss, and flagstone pavers make a bold artistic statement in this nearly plan view.

2.

Sasaki Associates
Watertown, Massachusetts

Planting was provided at every other level connecting the very top of the atrium space with the ground plane.

The Hercules building interior features a large, central, thirteen-story atrium surrounded by office floors. The atrium provides Hercules employees with a visual identity and focal point, and welcomes the public with an inviting walk through the building to the riverfront park. A large water sculpture is immediately visible from the south plaza entrance on Market Street. The north atrium glass wall faces Fletcher Brown Park. The main atrium floor is 60 feet by 100 feet (18.3 meters by 30.5 meters), stepping down from the south plaza main entrance to the north lounge spaces, a grade change of 20 feet (6.1 meters).

The multistory core of the atrium, with escalator connectors, provides spatial excitement when contrasted with the lower ceilings in foyers and adjoining lounges. The space is embellished by a central water runnel whose falls and basins step down through the interior garden planting. The atrium core faces north across Fletcher Brown Park and the Brandywine Creek area. Plantings include three specimen Weeping Fig trees (Ficus benjamina), espaliered plants at columns and walls, and seasonal flower displays. At the atrium's sides are 100-foot (30.5-meter), vine-covered stucco columns and planters, serving as treillage between the adjacent offices and atrium garden.

1.

2.

3.

4.

5.

1., 2., 3. Narrow pedestrian ways passing through the atrium connect street grade to park grade.

4. Irrigation and drainage was provided for each plant colony to assure survival and growth. A cabling system provides a safety net for maintenance personnel and maximizes views of the plant material from the atrium.

5. The Hercules building atrium, at the center of the new building mass, enjoys an urban frontage as well as a park frontage connecting the downtown and the Brandy-wine River. A cross street was closed, providing a direct connection of the atrium and the new park.

Joe Karr & Associates
Chicago, Illinois

Ameritech Center Corporate Headquarters
HOFFMAN ESTATES, ILLINOIS

The Ameritech Center is the headquarters for a five-state telecommunications corporation on a lushly landscaped 237-acre (95.9-hectare) site. The three-story building and its two adjoining garden-like parking structures are sensitively set in an expansive landscape of ponds, lakes, wetlands, formal gardens, courtyards, and rolling earthforms. When completed in 1992, the complex consolidated five divisions formerly working in nine different locations.

Inside, the 2,600 employees share a working environment focused on a generous and continuous network of pleasant, interconnected common space. Two flanking three-story atria, located at circulation nodes, are observable from great intersecting interior distances. The interior focal point is the skylighted central dining garden, which provides seating for hundreds of employees beneath overhanging trees.

The 1.3-million-square-foot (120,770-square-meter) facility includes an employee cafeteria, conference, health, and fitness centers, library, gift shops, beauty facilities, and ATM banking. With all the conveniences at hand, employees spend break times efficiently by

1.

2.

1. Pink Urn Plant *(Aechmea fasciata)* is one of twenty annual floral plant changes in the tiered planters. Foster Peperomia *(Pepperomia fosteri)* and Creeping Fig *(Ficus pumila)* are permanent ground covers in adjacent planters and in planters under the Weeping Podocarpus *(Podocarpus gracilior)*.

2. At opposite sides of each nodal atrium, raised planters with dense copses of 40-foot (12.2-meter) Native Bamboo *(Bambusa vulgarus aereovariegatus)* emerge from a bed of black Mexican pebbles. Open offices allow employees to look into the branches and touch the leaves from three floor levels.

3. Tiered planters with permanent ground covers and changing floral plants divide dining areas. Banks of supplemental down lights provide the high foot-candle levels needed by the Weeping Podocarpus *(Podocarpus gracilior)*.

remaining on the property. Exterior landscaping preserves the site's natural wetlands and maintains the environmental integrity of the existing property. Interior landscaping mimics the outdoors, bringing the natural features of the outside landscape into the heart of the building.

3.

Matt A. Bird, Diversifolia, Inc.
St. Louis, Missouri

Anheuser Busch Headquarters
ST. LOUIS, MISSOURI

The presence of water as an existing design element offered an opportunity to create the illusion of floating plants. This was done by using polished-brass bowls mounted on stands set to the identical depth as the water, with the base of the bowls just touching the water's surface.

At the opposite end of the lobby from the water feature is a triangular, in-ground planting bed, for which a 20-foot (6.1-meter) Norfolk Island Pine (*Araucaria excelsa*) was found. Once this large specimen was tagged, the underplantings used were Lily Turf (*Liriope* spp.), Cast Iron Plant (*Aspidistra elatior*), and a combination of seasonal bloomers and Bromeliads. This provided a natural, meadow-like feel; something similar to the grasses, pines, and flowers one might see in the neighboring Missouri countryside.

1.

1. A close-up shows how the use of Big Blue Lily-Turf *(Liriope muscari)*, Australian Tree Fern *(Alsophila australis)*, and Cast Iron Plant *(Aspidistra elatior)* combine to look very much like a meadow. The seasonals are changed every two weeks.

2. A 14,000-gallon (53,200-liter) pond is the focal point of this large lobby. Water was considered an essential part of this design effort, and floating floral arrangements and Hawaiian Orchids *(Dendrobium* spp.*)* made a real splash.

3. Creating the illusion of floating plants was an integral part of this design effect. A great deal of color is used to brighten and soften the lobby.

2.

3.

Ford Foundation Building
NEW YORK, NEW YORK

The garden of the Ford Foundation Building was the world's first large-scale, permanent interior landscape in a commercial building. Design began in 1964; the building opened in December 1967. As an original work of landscape art, the design concept was largely experimental. Lacking a background in building ventilation systems to support plants in a commercial building, designers assumed that winter temperatures in the atrium would not support tropical plants. Southern temperate plants were thus selected; the largest were eight matched Southern Magnolia *(Magnolia grandiflora)* with 14-inch (36-centimeter) caliper trunks, 9-ton (8,165-kilogram) root balls, and crown heights of 35 feet (10.7 meters). Others included Red Ironbark *(Eucalyptus sideroxylon)*, Sharpleaf Jacaranda *(Jacaranda acutifolia)*, and Japanese Cryptomeria *(Cryptomeria japonica 'Lobbi')*. Many of the other 999 shrubs, 148 vines, 21,954 ground covers, and eighteen aquatic plants were likewise atypical.

Winter temperatures turned out to be maintainable very close to spring, summer, and fall averages; and the southern plant palette was

1.

2.

4.

1. The grand stairway, looking up toward 43rd Street.

2. Four of the original Magnolia Trees *(Magnolia grandiflora)* remain in this view from the 12th floor, taken about 1981.

3. A plan view in 1994 shows the bright green canopies of Weeping Fig trees *(Ficus benjamina)*.

4. A long plan view from 1976.

3.

gradually replaced with tropicals. The last Magnolia was replaced in 1984. Despite the comprehensive species change, the visual concept has remained constant, and the project continues to be an oasis amid the concrete, steel, and glass of New York City.

1.

2.

1. A grove of Weeping Fig trees *(Ficus benjamina)* cast their shadows across the main stairway (1994).

2. Looking through dense underplantings and Ficus foliage towards the grand stairway.

3. Pointsettias *(Euphorbia pulcherimma)* line the main stairway rising from 42nd Street to 43rd Street during the holiday season.

3.

1.

2.

4.

3.

1. A 1976 ground-cover detail showing (clockwise from left) Kangaroo Vine *(Cissus antarctica)*, Coral Berry *(Ardisia crispa)*, Holly Fern *(Cyrtomium falcatum)*, and Variegated Japanese Pittosporum *(Pittosporum Tobira 'Variegata')*.

2. A walkway steps down to the southeast, towards a twelve-story curtain wall of glazing (1976).

3. Similar view as photo 2, eighteen years later. Note the visual similarities.

4. A different view of the same walkway looking back to the northwest.

5. The massive trunk of one of the original Magnolias *(Magnolia grandiflora)* sits to the right of a grouping of Bird's Nest Fern *(Asplenium nidus)* in 1976.

5.

1.

2.

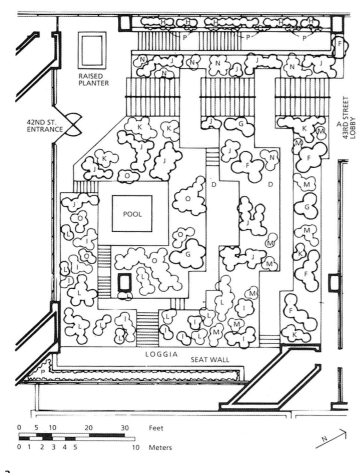

1. The reflecting pool had been altered by 1984 to contain a center planting of Peace Lily (Spathiphyllum sp.)

2. The foliage of the last remaining Magnolia (Magnolia grandiflora) arches into the frame from the right side.

3. An original plan of the shrub plantings.

4. An original plan of the ground-cover plantings.

3.

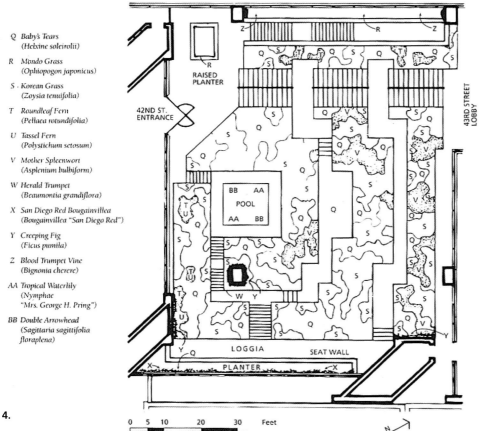

4.

CIGNA

BLOOMFIELD, CONNECTICUT

The Connecticut campus of CIGNA received a major addition in 1984 with a new 570,000-square-foot (52,953-square-meter) office building featuring a 470-foot (143.5-meter) landscaped atrium. While considered an important visual amenity of the building, the atrium and its large glass roof were conceived principally as an energy-conscious design element, introducing significant amounts of natural daylight into adjoining office space and reducing the need for electric lighting. The ancillary benefits to plantings are obvious, with a high level of diffused lighting available to the majority of plants in the space.

1.

2.

3.

4.

5.

1. An upper-level view contrasts the dense foliage of the Weeping Fig trees *(Ficus benjamina)* with the open foliage of the Black Olive trees (*Bucida buceras*).

2. A grouping of Fan Palms *(Livistona chinensis)* provides a distinct textural quality at the top of the escalators.

3. A variety of foliage textures and shapes is overshadowed by the hemispherical spikes of a large Screw Pine *(Pandanus Veitchii)* at the base of the waterfall.

4. Two columnar Sourthern Yew (Podocarpus macrophyllus) stand in front of a grove of Weeping Fig trees *(Ficus benjamina)*.

5. Massed Wallis Peace Lily *(Spathiphyllum 'Wallisii')* are used as ground cover in the foreground of the water feature.

National Fire Protection Association Headquarters
QUINCY, MASSACHUSETTS

This interior landscape offers visitors a dramatic setting for the main lobby entry to the building. An active stream of water spills down and meanders under a canopy of trees. A stepping-stone path leads visitors through the garden, allowing them to interact with the boulders, fish, and waterfalls. The floor-to-ceiling south-facing glass wall framing the south side of the garden provides sunlight for both healthy plant growth and light contrast along the waterway. The glass wall also allows the exterior to commingle with the interior landscape, effectively enlarging the lobby to include the adjacent plantings outdoors.

1.

2.

1. The upper-level entrance to the garden begins with stone cut to seem like it is growing out of the concrete floor of the building.

2. By its placement against the window wall, the interior garden becomes an extension of the garden outside the lobby

3. Overlooking the garden, visitors are offered a dramatic view of the main waterfall and lower Koi pool at the base of the garden. Note how the small planting of seasonals in the lower right corner of each photograph immediately catches the eye.

3.

1.

1. This is a view of the garden during the construction and setting of the boulders and streamway. You can see the way the stones are set in order to define and contain both the plant beds and the stream.

2. This comprehensive view from the first and second floors show the dramatic impact of the multilevel garden.

3. The view down the third-floor mezzanine picks up the contrasting textures of the Weeping Fig *(Ficus benjamina)* and Neanthe Bella Palm *(Chamaedorea elegans)* foliage.

2.

3.

Larry M. Pliska, Planterra Tropical Greenhouses Inc.
West Bloomfield, Michigan

Insignia Commercial Group
BINGHAM FARMS, MICHIGAN

This is a renovation of a four-story office atrium complex completed after a change of ownership. The new owners requested a park setting with intimate spaces. Precast concrete panel walkways and park benches were installed to achieve the desired look. A combination of 15-foot to 20-foot (4.6-meter to 6.1-meter) Weeping Fig trees *(Ficus benjamina)* were used as a counterpoint to groupings of sculptured 6-foot to 7-foot (1.8-meter to 2.1-meter) Dwarf Janet Craig Dracaena *(Dracaena deremensis 'Janet Craig Compacta')*. A multitude of flowering plants and mixed ground covers complete the indoor park environment.

2.

1.

1. Groups of exotic Bromeliads *(Neoregelia spp.)* add color to the landscape.

2. A view from the atrium entrance shows the scope of the project.

[opposite] Park benches enhance the outdoor feeling of the space.

Carey Baker
Highland, Michigan

LDM Technologies, Inc.
AUBURN HILLS, MICHIGAN

An intimate and inviting plant-filled environment was created in the 5,000-square-foot (464.5-square-meter) atrium lobby of a high-tech automotive manufacturing company. During the design phase, focus was placed on design details such as form and texture. Smaller material such as Anthurium *(Anthurium* spp.*)*, Prayer Plant *(Maranta* spp.*)*, and Peperomia *(Peperomia* spp.*)* provides interest through a variety in texture and color. An oversized Weeping Fig tree *(Ficus benjamina)* was selected as a focal specimen. Its mature-looking trunk was sought to provide additional interest. Foliage was then pruned to proportion the tree to its space. Bromeliads are perched within Spanish Moss *(Tillandsia useneiodes)* in the trunk of the tree. Trees are underplanted with Birds' Nest Fern *(Asplenium nidus)*, Hooker's Anthurium *(Anthurium 'Hookeri')*, and Calathea *(Calathea* spp.*)*. A variety of colorful ground covers are featured, with a specimen King Sago Palm *(Cycas revoluta)* included for a low-level textural contrast. A wall of 12-foot (3.7-meter) Bamboo adjacent to a 15-foot (4.6-meter) Weeping Fig tree *(Ficus benjamina)* underplanted with flowering Peace Lily *(Spathiphyllum* spp.*)* creates an inviting walkway.

1.

2.

4.

3.

1. This bird's-eye view of the atrium lobby focuses on a 20-foot (6.1-meter) Alexander Palm *(Ptychosperma elegans)* in the foreground and yellow Chrysanthemums *(Chrysanthemum spp.)* in the background.

2. A row of 12-foot Bamboo along the curtain wall on the left is juxtaposed with 15-foot (4.6-meter) Weeping Fig trees *(Ficus benjamina)* under-planted with flowering Peace Lilies *(Spathiphyllum spp.)* to create an inviting walkway.

3. A sunken circle of dark granite paving is separated from the higher surrounding paving with low plantings, while trees and palms fill the rest of the space.

4. An unusual specimen Weeping Fig *(Ficus benjamina)*, displaying many aerial roots along its trunk, is made even more exotic with perched Bromeliads and Spanish Moss *(Tillandsia useneoides)* in its branches. The tree is under-planted with Bird's Nest Fern *(Asplenium nidus)*, Hooker's Anthurium *(Anthurium 'Hookerii')*, and Zebra Plant *(Calathea zebrina)*.

Matt A. Bird, Diversifolia, Inc.
St. Louis, Missouri

Sterling Direct
ST. LOUIS, MISSOURI

The president of Sterling Direct offered a few key words as a directive for the interior landscape: "Woodsy. Natural. Northwest."

The design concept began with the use of fiberglass planters. To provide an unusual touch, the planters were placed on black cold rolled-steel pedestals. Norfolk Island Pine (*Araucaria heterophylla*) was the first step in creating the desired look. Alocasia and Calathea were used to match the interior finishes and bring out the woodsy feel of forest undergrowth. Different varieties of ferns and Lily Turf (*Liriope* spp.) further enhanced the concept. Dried fungus, of the type used in floral arrangements, was fastened to the trunk of the Pine, and Spanish Moss (*Tillandsia useneoides*) was delicately draped from the branches. The plants were then top-dressed with Sphagnum Moss.

1.

2.

1. Detail shows how the textures of Fern Big Blue Lily Turf (*Liriope muscari*) provide an interesting combination. Calathea (*Calathea* spp.) and Elephant's Ear Plant (*Alocasia* sp.) tie in the surrounding colors.

2. Detail of the one of the combination planters displaying a rich mixture of color and texture in a confined space.

[opposite] Grasses, Ferns, and a big Norfolk Island Pine (*Araucaria heterophylla*) create a woodsy look. Black metal stands and green fiberglass add elegance to the space.

Brown Forman Forester Center
LOUISVILLE, KENTUCKY

The renovated Whisky Storage Warehouse with a skylit atrium of inverted ziggurat form supplies most of the light for the office building. The soaring interior space creates an invigorating work environment for the six floors of open offices surrounding it.

Upon entering the space, one is greeted by a lushly landscaped scene supplemented by a triangular-stepped waterfall. Bamboo trees provide a 40-foot (12.2-meter) height scale in the 100-foot-tall (30.5-meter-tall) space. The drop-column panels on the perimeter of the space provide a logical place for additional planters at each level of the atrium.

The preservation and exposure of the heavy concrete columns and column caps express the historic character of the building, while recalling its previous use as a six-floor whisky barrel storage area.

1.

2.

1. Column-top planters extend the garden to the upper-office floors above the canopy of the bamboo trees that rise from the garden below.

2. Hanging Lipstick Plant *(Aeschynanthus lobbianus)* overlooks the gardens terrace levels with massings of Bears Breach *(Acanthus mollis)*, Amazon Lily *(Eucharis grandiflora)*, Boston Fern *(Nephrolepis exaltata 'Bostoniensis')* and Creeping Fig *(Ficus pumila)* from which new Native Bamboo shoots continue to sprout and grow.

3. Lipstick Plant *(Aeschynanthus lobbianus)*, with its profuse red flowers, hangs gently over the edge of upper planters. Lady Jane Anthurium *(Anthurium 'Lady Jane')* provides larger leaf contrast.

3.

Joe Karr & Associates
Chicago, Illinois

Trans Am

OAKBROOK TERRACE, ILLINOIS

Trans Am Plaza is a speculative office-building complex consisting of two identical five-story buildings on a lavishly landscaped site. Each building has a full height skylighted central atrium as its centerpiece. Each soaring open interior space not only provides natural light to inner offices, but also offers a lush, green, living environment inside the building throughout the otherwise dull winter months. The cheery presence of each atrium has proven to be a positive amenity in the successful leasing of office space.

1.

2.

3.

4.

1. The elegant simplicity of the skylight is ever present through the foliage of the Weeping Fig trees *(Ficus benjamina)* in the garden.

2. Glass elevators carry office personnel and visitors up through the garden atmosphere to all floors. The appearance of the five stories of plantings is different at each level.

3. Multistem Weeping Fig trees *(Ficus benjamina)* form an enclosing canopy at the ground-floor level. Hawaiian Schefflera *(Schefflera arboricola)* and Japanese Fatsia *(Fatsia japonica)* shrubs emerge in clusters from the Peace Lilies *(Spathiphyllum 'Mauna Loa')* and Algerian Ivy *(Hedera canariensis)* groundcover matrix.

4. The dense, flowing, exterior landscape, in which parking areas are hidden and roadways softly pass by the buildings, sets the stage for the bright landscape surprise inside each building.

BUILDING 1:
Michael Singer, Wilmington, Vermont
Michael McKinnell, Kallmann McKinnell & Wood
Boston, Massachusetts
Morgan Wheelock, Somerville, Massachusetts

BUILDING 2:
Kallmann McKinnell & Wood Architects
Boston, Massachusetts
Morgan Wheelock, Somerville, Massachusetts

Becton Dickinson Headquarters
FRANKLIN LAKES, NEW JERSEY

Becton Dickinson and Company (BD), one of the world's largest manufacturers of medical devices, is a company of knowledgeable workers. The client wanted to create for its employees a serene working environment that would encourage human interaction and help promote the exchange of ideas. Architects Kallmann McKinnell & Wood responded with a three-building master plan crafted for the rolling hillsides of BD's 14-acre (5.6-hectare) wooded site in Franklin Lakes, New Jersey. To date, two of the three planned buildings have been designed and constructed and together form a suburban corporate campus that incorporates over 800,000 square feet (72,000 square meters) of offices, laboratories, and support spaces. In 1990 and 1998, the two buildings separately received the AIA Honor Award for Architecture.

BD's workplaces are organized on the perimeters of large wings that, in plan, resemble the fingers of a hand stretching out over a great lawn. The effect is to give every worker views of the woodland setting. The two buildings, which are only three stories high, step down into the landscape allowing easy access to the trees, benches, gardens,

1.

2.

and works of environmental art outside. Nature is brought inside as well. At the center of each wing, offices face inward to a triple-height sunlit atrium. For each atrium, a separate interior landscape was created using plant life, water, earth, and stone.

1. Atrium #2 in Building II is an aquatic garden that has been innovatively installed in only 12 inches (31 cm) of crater. The 34-foot-high (10.4-meter-high) sculptural figure is of Japanese origin and reflects the clients' commitment to a global perspective.

2. Atrium #3 in Building II is a planted bamboo court for quiet meditation and relaxation. It is visually and spatially connected directly to the outdoors—offering an extension of the natural landscape into the work environment.

3. Atrium #1 in Building I is naturally lit by large clerestory windows and is open to three floors of office, dining, and conference facilities. The planted sculpture garden is a collaborative effort between Michael Singer (artist) and Michael McKinnell (architect).

3.

Hospitality

The atrium concept as a public space within the walls of a building dates back to Roman times, but its transformation into a multistory indoor hotel space was introduced in 1967 with John Portman's Hyatt Regency Hotel in Atlanta, and soon afterwards at Portman's Embarcadero Hyatt Hotel in San Francisco.

In the years since, the hotel atrium has made increasingly more inventive and grander use of plants to liven the spaces in which they are placed. Wider expanses of skylighting, coupled with advances in glazing design that allow for better light control, provide a more pleasant, natural aura while increasing light availability for plant growth without the need for cumbersome and expensive plant-growth lights. Not coincidentally, the natural lighting of a large atrium also reduces other electric-lighting needs during daylight hours.

Embassy Suites Hotel:
The fronds of the Wine Palms *(Caryota urens)* are supplemented with smaller palms at eye level *(Fishtail Palms-Caryota mitis; Kentia Palms-Howeia forsterana)* and other lush underplantings to provide a decidedly tropical environment.

Many hotel atria combine the soothing effects of natural lighting and plants with the refreshing sights and sounds of moving water and the textural complexities of artificial rock formations to create comprehensive environments closely approximating those outside the hotel's walls, or exotic environments thousands of miles away.

This section illustrates some of the more innovative uses of interior landscaping in the public spaces of hotels and inns.

Hyatt Regency Greenwich
GREENWICH, CONNECTICUT

The Hyatt Regency Greenwich atrium, created to resemble an exterior Connecticut landscape, offers a tremendous variety of interior landscape plant materials and water features. Throughout the atrium and restaurants are many interesting groupings of exotic foliage, including a 25-foot (7.6-meter) Eucalyptus *(Eucalyptus sp.)*, and Amazon Lilies *(Eucharis grandifolia)* in constant flower due to the high levels of light. Gardenias *(Gardenia jasmanoides)* are also in flower, providing a wonderful aroma. A rock wall has been placed on the hillside along the water feature, with large Liriope Grass, Boston Ferns, and a seasonal flower rotation. The lawn is sod, mowed with an electric lawn mower to eliminate pollution, and specially grown to tolerate lower light levels.

1.

3.

1. The vigorous Creeping Fig *(Ficus pumila)* encircles the columns, giving even the peripheral portions of the atrium a feeling of lushness.

2. The rapid vertical growth of the Creeping Fig *(Ficus pumila)* is evident as the green portions of the columns continue to rise.

3. With the skylights of the atrium blocked from view by the overhanging foliage of Fig trees, this interior space looks convincingly like an outdoor scene.

2.

Robert Shaheen, Landscape Associates
Little Rock, Arkansas

Crown Center Hotel
KANSAS CITY, MISSOURI

The design and construction of the Crown Center Hotel evolved over a period of six years (1968–1973), on a very difficult site—the former Signboard Hill, a steep slope of limestone and shale on which were placed many old billboards. The interior garden is constructed on the slope itself, an environment not easy to build on or maintain. The garden is 120 feet (36.6 meters) long by 80 feet (24.4 meters) wide and has a soil depth of 18 inches (46 cm) except for the trees, which are in pits excavated from the shale.

An important concept was the naturalization of this inner environment to be complementary to the exterior environment around Kansas City. The stream bed had to be reconstituted to make it appear to be in a natural environment here. To do that, three to four feet of shale was excavated and replaced with the natural limestone found in nearby areas to simulate the stream bed. Many of the rocks, some of which ranged up to 15 tons (13,500 kilograms) in size, were lowered through the metal roof beams before the skylight was put in. They helped make the slope as natural looking as possible, and also helped retard erosion of planted areas down the hillside.

1.

2.

3.

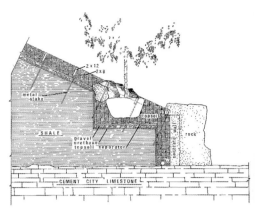

4.

Plant material selections were intended to be very much like native types. The Weeping Fig trees *(Ficus benjamina)* were selected for their resemblance to the river birch trees that grow wild in this area. Many ferns were used to replicate the ferns in nearby woods. Baby's Tears (*Soleirolia soleirolii*) was used as a simulation of moss for a dwarf ground cover.

One of the rare things about this space not available in many other projects is a series of eight vantage points from which to observe the garden, a wonderful opportunity for visitors.

1. Walkway to stream showing adding membrane and tree pits and rock placement, 1972.

2. A view almost straight down from the upper garden level shows the amount of attention paid to the use of ground covers in the space.

3. The walkway crosses the stream bed amid rocks interspersed with ferns.

4. Technique for hillside stabilization, 1972.

Marriott's Orlando World Center
ORLANDO, FLORIDA

The architecture and interior landscape of the Orlando World Center establish transitional indoor-outdoor relationships that enhance the resort experience of this first-class hotel. In the lobby arrival area, layered plant material gradually exposes guests to the interior architecture as they progress to the expansive glass atrium. The first layer of low branching Fig trees underplanted with bold seasonal color, creates a comfortable human-scaled arrival. Beyond the Fig trees, 30- to 40- foot (9- to 12- meter) Queen Palms *(Syagrus Romanzoffianum)* soar upward into the atrium surrounding the central grand stair leading to ballrooms below. From the center of the atrium, views to the lobby bar and beyond to the pools are framed by Adonidia Palms *(Veitchia Merrillii)* and large Bird of Paradise plants *(Strelitzia nicolai).*

The ballroom prefunction areas combine water and plantings to create intimate seating areas for small groups. Color is used at the water's edge to take advantage of its reflective quality. The space is designed to accommodate a variety of different group sizes, from small, intimate gatherings to large numbers of conference attendees.

1.

2.

5.

1. Central Atrium at entry from Porte Cochere.

2. Lush plantings and water features provide an intimate setting for guests before or after ballroom functions.

3. Integrating planting with signage strengthens the exotic theme for this restaurant.

4. Prefunction area: the at-grade planters shown here resemble the exterior planters just beyond this photo.

5. Central Atrium space and Grand Stair to meeting rooms at lower level. The entry is flanked by Fig trees with Queen Palms *(Syagrus Romanzoffianum)* beyond accentuating the verticality of the space.

3.

4.

Denise Breitfuss, Rentokil
Riverwoods, Illinois

Wyndham Hotel
ITASCA, ILLINOIS

A magnificent twelve-story atrium comprises the central core of this upscale hotel in Chicago's northwestern suburbs. The lobby, registration, restaurant, lounge, and deli are all centralized within the hotel's atrium. Each function area is separated and defined by the use of interior plantings. A formal seating area flanking the front registration desk is softened by freestanding containers of Kentia Palms *(Howea Forsterana)*. Adjacent to the seating area are ten large Indian Laurel Fig trees *(Ficus nitida)*. The canopy of the Indian Laurel Fig trees provides shade for café tables where patrons dine on sandwiches from the adjacent deli. Foliage within marble-clad planters camouflages the mechanical equipment of the atrium's beautiful glass elevators. Guests enjoy the breathtaking view of the tropical palms and colorful foliage only from within the elevator. The atrium's sunken lounge is concealed by a series of tiered planters that ensure privacy. Eye-level plantings provide both visual and audible screening for patrons dining at adjacent tables.

1.

2.

3.

1. Four thousand Pothos *(Epipremnum aureum)* form a uniform, dense hedge in balcony planters on each of the twelve stories overlooking the atrium.

2. This bird's-eye view show the openness of the atrium. Note the planters that surround the sunken lounge beneath an elaborate Asian canopy.

3. Vibrant color is achieved beneath the palms by integrating the reds, yellows, and oranges of Croton *(Codiaeum* sp.) with yellow and green variegated Hawaiian Schefflera *(Schefflera arboricola 'Variegata').*

Embassy Suites Hotel
PARSIPPANY, NEW JERSEY

The goal of the interior landscape design for the Embassy Suites in Parsippany, New Jersey was to create a park-like setting that was both fun and enjoyable for the corporate user as well as for families.

Soft colors and materials were used in creating the space. An enormous amount of terra-cotta colored brick patterns, as well as water and rock work, were used. Several thousand plants, from ground-cover ivies to 25-foot (7.6-meter) Weeping Fig trees (Ficus benjamina), as well as hanging plants in balcony planters, were used to soften architectural edges and surfaces. High-intensity lighting supplement the skylights that were installed to ensure the longevity of the exotic palms and trees in the atrium. Several hundred cubic yards of specially prepared planting medium was installed for proper root growth. Flowering plants are in bloom year-round providing both color and excitement.

1.

2.

3.

1. An overall view shows the vast size and scope of the atrium landscaping

2. A view of the main atrium.

3. A look at the atrium from the main entrance. The planter consists of Silver Queen Chinese Evergreen (*Aglaonema 'Silver Queen'*) and a seasonal flower rotation.

James Martin Associates
Vernon Hills, Illinois

Embassy Suites Hotel
DEERFIELD, ILLINOIS

The 300-room all-suites hotel serves the affluent North Shore suburban community of Chicago. The hotel has a seven story atrium whose elaborate landscaping brings a tropical flavor to the property. Specimen palms and ornamental trees are used in combination with pools of water, small waterfalls, and winding walkways. The entire planting is directly planted in the ground. This allows larger trees to reach full maturity and the understory plants to proliferate in a natural garden effect. The building's design makes excellent use of overhead skylights to create a dramatic effect of light penetrating through the canopy of foliage. Planting is lush and full, with a variety of color and texture. Ground covers spread along the edge of stream beds and climb over the rock boulders. The soft texture of graceful, arching palms sweeps gently across the walkway. A dense planting of Pothos (*Epipremnum aureum*) cascades from the balcony railings which overlook the garden.

1.

2.

1. Winding walkways invite guests to enter the lush vegetation of the atrium. The graceful foliage of palm trees creates a canopy over secluded seating areas along the walkway.

2. A second level view displays a wide variety of interesting horticultural textures, the result of specifying many different species for each area of the atrium.

3.

4.

3. The long, graceful fronds of a Kentia Palm *(Howea forsterana)* arch over dense understory plantings and rocks.

4. The use of living greenery is continued above the atrium floor with balcony plantings of Jade Pothos *(Epipremnum aureum 'Tropic Green').*

Steve McCurdy, Landscape Images
Lake Forest, California

1.

The Embassy Suites Hotel in La Jolla, California, was built in 1987, and underwent a major, phased renovation that began in 1995. All the planters in the atrium were renovated one at a time, leaving the Wine Palms *(Caryota urens)* as the only surviving plants from the original installation, and even they were transplanted, having been planted initially in their own growing containers. The renovation included the removal of much of the existing hardpan clay substrate, which caused many of the original plantings to suffer from water stress. The Wine Palms were augmented with several species of smaller palms to help relate the older specimens to their newer counterparts. The profusion of palm trees and dense understory shrubs and grounds covers create an inviting tropical setting in the lobby. Liberal use of color is made in both permanent and seasonal plantings to enhance the decor of the lobby all year round.

2.

1. An overview of the atrium illustrates the extent of landscaping and water features in the floor plan.

2. In a view looking down from the top floor, the fronds of a grove of Wine Palms *(Caryota urens)* form a bold textural statement in one corner of the atrium.

[opposite] This ground-level shot shows the degree to which the natural and built environments are interrelated in a hotel lobby.

The Emerald Shapery Center/Pan Pacific Hotel
SAN DIEGO, CALIFORNIA

This large twenty-nine-story premiere corporate hotel and office complex is tied together by a soaring nine-story, 100-foot (30.5-meter) atrium. The building is a series of eight hexagonal-shaped towers, ranging from eighteen to thirty stories in height, and this hexagonal theme is evident throughout the building, right down to the shape of the planters. The interior landscape contractors were consulted on this project almost three years before the installation, but there were still some areas where the planters were too small due to mechanical and engineering obstructions running through them.

The entire project is installed on the Mona sub-irrigation system by utilizing the link system. Siphon tubes were also installed to facilitate the removal of excess water, especially on the exterior containers and planters. This project was designed with an extensive color program, but a Mona irrigation system was installed so that it could be easily converted to foliage irrigation if needed, which was the case with many projects during the 1991–1996 recession.

1.

2.

3.

1. Viewed from the second floor, the balcony plantings make as much of a visual impact on the space as the larger floor plants below.

2. This overall view of the lobby shows a number of ways to highlight the attributes of plants: Bromeliads display bright colors in the foreground, a Wine Palm *(Caryota urens)* displays an interesting habit of growth, and the hanging vines offer textural relief at the upper levels.

3. Palms *(Howea forsterana, Rhapis excelsa)* and Urn Plants *(Aechmea fasciata)* in dark granite planters frame the walkway to restaurant.

Institutional

The enhancement of interior spaces with living plants and creative design is as familiar in the world of hotels and shopping malls as it is in our homes and workplaces. Creative interior landscapes give a sense of purpose and place to institutions, which are an important part of our culture.

The role of the restorative garden as part of the healing process has a history extending back to the twelfth century. Professor Sam Bass Warner, of Brandeis University's Department of American Studies, suggests that our perception of gardens' curative power has ebbed and flowed over the centuries in successive waves of discovery and rediscovery. He writes that "when society as a whole thinks that Nature is a powerful force for human well-being, then gardens for patients appear in hospitals. When, on the other hand, the general society feels that its science and art can master Nature then the gardens disappear." At the end of the twentieth century, interior landscapes in hospitals, nursing homes, and other health-care facilities indicate a growing recognition of plants in the healing process.

Indoor gardens provide a link between the creation of nature and the human works of art in libraries, museums, and galleries. The creation of a peaceful atmosphere adds to the quiet contemplation of the masterpieces on display. Simple and restrained gardens provide a place where visitors can pause for reflection between viewings. Control of the environment for the protection of artworks takes priority over plants needs, with humidity and temperature levels usually lower than optimum for plants; and the choice of plant material and effective maintenance procedures are therefore crucial. The projects illustrated demonstrate the success of good design and proper planning in institutional milieux.

Beth Israel Hospital:

A traditional fluted light pole rises from within a bed of ground covers and low shrubs in one of several rectangular planters in the atrium.

London Standard Chartered Bank
LONDON, ENGLAND

The world headquarters of the London Standard Chartered Bank, in London's Financial District, houses a nine-story atrium that blends historical continuity with modern functionality and tropical exuberance. Fourteen specially grown Southern Magnolias (*Magnolia grandiflora*), a fountain, waterfalls and channels, plus lushly planted ground forms provide a respite from the often dreary London weather.

To maintain an ancient forty-five-degree pedestrian connection between Bishopgate and Threadneedle Street, the design combines octagonal shapes and changes of level to preserve an allusion to the original passageway.

At the building's main entrance from Bishopgate, office workers and bank customers are greeted by a late-Victorian marble statue from within a grove of tall, slender Magnolias.

An additional VIP entrance marks the beginning of one of two granite-walled canals that bisect and organize the atrium spaces. Through these angled flumes, water runs over smooth stones, falls alongside or flows under stairs marking level changes, and

1.

finally drops in two free-falling waterfalls into an octagonal cylinder. Windows from the lower-level restaurant give views of the waterfalls and pool. The other channel emanates from a fountain at the other side of the atrium, near the entrance from Crosby Square.

2.

1. Two bisecting granite-walled canals organize the atrium spaces. Through these angled flumes, water runs over smooth pebbles, falls alongside or flows under stairs, and drops in two free-falling waterfalls into an octagonal cylinder. Windows from the lower-level restaurant offer views of the waterfalls and pools.

2. A hemispherical fountain is visible through the foliage of a Southern Magnolia (*Magnolia grandiflora*).

3. Design sections through the multistory lobby atrium.

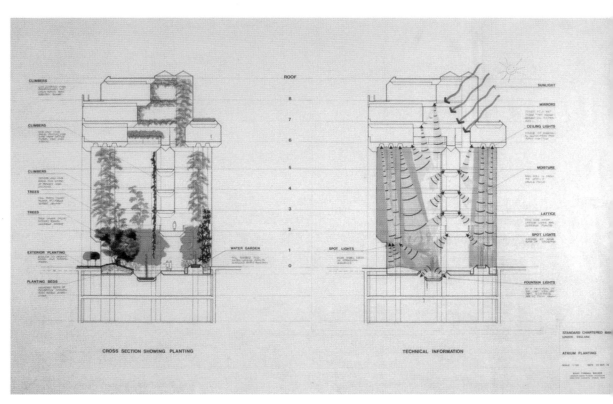

3.

Peter Hornbeck & Associates
North Andover, Massachusetts

Class of 1959 Chapel, Harvard Business School
CAMBRIDGE, MASSACHUSETTS

The Class of 1959 Chapel is a nondenominational sacred and meditative space. The cylindrical, green, oxidized copper drum intersects a glazed interior garden that terraces down into the earth. Biblical plants, flowering trees, and water form a transparent oasis in the heart of the campus, and create a quiet transition from daily to spiritual experience. A tower timepiece by artist Karl Schlamminger stands at the entry to the chapel, its gold sphere rising and falling twenty-four hours a day.

Inside, the one-hundred-seat sanctuary is contained by undulating banded concrete walls that rise to a height of 27 feet (8.2 meters). Multiple axes encourage any spatial orientation for worship, and since the chapel opened, exceptional acoustics have regularly drawn instrumental and vocal performers to fill the room with sound.

During the day, light enters the sanctuary from overhead. Within the skylights, large-scale acrylic prisms designed by Charles Ross are filled with mineral oil and positioned to refract sunlight and wash the walls with the colors of the visible spectrum. A rotating drum supports this array and follows the sun's path; as the sun moves across the sky, glowing patterns slowly move and change across the chapel walls.

1.

2.

1. The sloped glazing of the chapel enables the exterior planting and interior planting to become visually inter-twined.

2. The delicate architectural treatment of the stairs is echoed by the lacy foliage of the Rice Paper Plant *(Cyperus papyrus)* in the pool and the Bamboo on the right.

3. The Rice Paper Plant *(Cyperus papyrus)* produces distinctively different foliage than the surrounding plants, with a finer texture and a lighter green color.

3.

State of Illinois Revenue Center
SPRINGFIELD, ILLINOIS

The State of Illinois Revenue Center is a linear building covering three blocks in length, providing six floors of offices for 2,000 employees. The exterior site is heavily landscaped, but the main feature of the building's interior environment is a central atrium with all six office floors facing onto it. The atrium consists of a 700-foot-long (213.5-meter-long) landscaped space with a bridge/walkway system meandering down the entire length of the garden, crossing a continuously flowing stream at waterfall segments that drop approximately 16 feet (4.9 meters) in elevation cumulatively among terraced plantings to a pool.

Artificial lighting suspended from the skylight structure allows for a complex plant palette of subtropical plants to carpet the garden at all levels from which employees can experience the restful character of the landscape and the gentle sound of the flowing water.

1.

2.

4.

3.

1. A sloping skylight allows six stories of light to reach into the interior garden. Exterior terraced planters surrounding the site echo a complex system of planters in the interior garden.

2. Balconies at five floor levels provide numerous vantage points from which employees can view and experience the garden. A stepped metal walkway leads down into the garden.

3. Sculpture nodes provide rest stops along the full length of the garden.

4. Water spills over lannon-stone ledges as the meandering stream passes down through the garden among dense plantings of trees, shrubs, groundcovers and ferns.

Nelson R. Hammer, Hammer Design
Boston, Massachusetts

Memorial Health Care Building
WORCESTER, MASSACHUSETTS

The lobby of the new Memorial Health Care Building is the main pedestrian entrance to all buildings of the hospital's campus. As such, a substantial portion of the lobby space is devoted to seating and other visitor amenities. Integral to the amenities are eight matched Weeping Fig trees *(Ficus benjamina)* placed in tree grates in a single line down the center of the lobby, the scale of which is evident in the nighttime photo. Although some supplemental metal-halide lighting is provided to encourage top growth, the primary light source for the plants is the east-facing window glazing. With most light coming from an acute, low angle (morning sun), the trees were placed on turntables beneath the tree grates to allow them to be rotated and keep their symmetrical growth pattern.

1.

1. All eight of the lobby trees were placed on turntables that allow them to be rotated to receive light from the east-facing sidewall glazing. The trees are turned 90 degrees about once a month.

2. Five of the eight Weeping Fig trees *(Ficus benjamina)*—four on either side of the main entrance—are visible in this view down the length of the lobby.

3. The impact of the trees on the lobby is evident in this panoramic nighttime view.

2.

3.

Louise Schiller Associates
Princeton, New Jersey

LDR International
Columbia, Maryland

Situated on 22.5 acres (9 hectares), HHMI's 305,000-square-foot (27,450-square-meter) Headquarters and Conference Center consolidated the Institute's administrative and conferencing activities on one campus when it was dedicated in 1993. One of the key issues in designing the HHMI facility was to take advantage of the splendid site and create a rich dialogue between the buildings and the landscape. To foster a feeling of seclusion in a park-like setting and promote a relaxed, isolated atmosphere amid not only a residential area but also a number of heavily traveled thoroughfares, the designers limited access to the site and creatively utilized natural sound barriers and existing vegetation. Brick, wood, and stone building materials complement the natural setting, and low-profile buildings create a residential atmosphere throughout the campus.

The headquarters is organized around a series of landscaped courtyards providing natural light and view to every office. Flanking the west-facing main entrance, the tall rotunda of the campus library stands as a symbol of the Institute. Just beyond the entrance, the skylit conservatory anchors the headquarters.

1.

2.

quarters. By day it is the piazza, or living room of the Institute. Lanterns in concrete brackets and spotlights on the steel roof trusses offer subdued lighting for evening function. With Plumbago Vines *(plumbago* sp.*)* covering the full height of the perimeter columns, the conservatory is truly an enclosed portion of the landscaped campus.

1. View across the Conservatory into an open courtyard. Natural light and landscape enter the room through the walls. English greenstone on the floor symbolizes the flow of lawn into the room

2. The unusual foliage of Bird-of-Paradise *(Strelitzia nicolai)* was selected as the feature planting for the wood planter boxes in the center of the atrium.

3. Plumbago Vine *(plumbago* sp.*)* now covers the original wire supports. Wooden garden benches and planters reinforce the strong visual connection between outside and inside.

3.

Phillips Ambulatory Care Center, Beth Israel Hospital
NEW YORK, NEW YORK

This outpatient clinic was constructed from a renovated office space. The focal point of the building is a four story atrium with a park-like setting, and light poles were specified that resemble those found in a park outside the building. Four specimen trees and more than six hundred understory plantings fill the space. Because drainage from the planters was not possible, subirrigation units were installed to minimize the possibility of water build-up. The atrium contains a series of planter boxes and balcony plantings with a park-like design theme and features 10-foot (3-meter) to 12-foot (3.7-meter) Alii Fig trees (*Ficus 'Alii'*), Variegated Hawaiian Schefflera (*Schefflera arboricola 'Variegata'*), Wallis Peace Lily (*Spathiphyllum 'Wallisi'*) Self-Heading Philodendron (*Philodendron selloum*), Neanthe Bella Palms (*Chamaedorea elegans*), Emerald Beauty Chinese Evergreen (*Aglaonema 'Emerald Beauty'*), Arrowhead Vine (*Syngonium podophyllum*). As daylight winds downs, the street lights illuminate the atrium.

1.

2.

1. Three rectangular planters repeat a theme of trees, shrubs, and street lights.

2. In this overall photo, several 20-foot by 8-foot (6.1-meter by 2.4 meter) planters at the lower level are augmented by a variety of low plantings at the base of the handrail at the mezzanine above.

Pierpont Morgan Library
NEW YORK, NEW YORK

The Garden Court of the Pierpont Morgan Library occupies the link between the original library and an addition built in 1990–1991 on property that formerly contained a house in which J. P. Morgan Jr. lived until his death in 1943, and a garden designed by noted landscape architect Beatrix Farrand during the 1920s. The court was meant to have the feel of an English conservatory or of a French jardin des plantes, while also perpetuating the spirit of Farrand's garden. It provides a bright, airy, public space that has proven to be a most pleasant place for receptions, dinners, and concerts. Five Black Olive trees *(Bucida spinosa 'Shady Lady')* are the major horticultural elements, but there exists a fascinating variety of smaller scale genera within the court.

1.

2.

3.

1. Creeping Fig *(Ficus pumila)* grows vigorously up the stone walls of the Garden Room.

2. Boston Fern *(Nephrolepis exaltata 'Bostoniensis')* is used as an underplanting beneath the Black Olive trees *(Bucida buceras)*, and Baby's Tears *(Soleirolia soleirolii)* is planted directly beneath the trees.

3. The massive canopies of the Black Olive trees *(Bucida buceras)* fill one side of the Garden Room.

Residential

Nature and culture are inextricably entwined. From classical times to modern, from Europe to Asia, interior decoration has brought the most pleasing features of the natural world indoors. This relationship has been determined primarily by climate; gardens of the past were a vital extension of the delights of spring and summer. The merging of living space with the garden and the wider landscape fulfilled a deep-seated need to relate directly with nature—a need that derives from the evolutionary roots of our existence.

In direct contrast to the housing of much of our civilized history, modern residences benefit enormously from lighting, heating, plumbing, and glazing that provide comfort and protection from climate and weather. The sophistication of present urban living has separated us from the natural environment; yet the need for close contact with green plants remains.

Our ability to bring the outdoors in is greatly enhanced by modern residential design, construction, and materials: skylights to flood our rooms with sunlight; efficient insulation and heating; ventilating and air-conditioning systems that the eliminate drafts and hot spots that had previously spelled doom for indoor plantings.

Increasing interest in the environment and ecology has heightened enthusiasm for gardening, and as in Roman times, the garden as an extension of the house has returned as the functional "garden room." Conversely, plants fill nooks and crannies not intended for greenery at all.

A wide palette of flowering plants, colorful foliage, and sculpturally attractive species have been horticulturally adapted to thrive indoors, and many have found their way into our homes. Interior designers are recognizing the need to be in contact with the natural world—to maintain the living link with our origins. As this chapter shows, this need can be fulfilled in our own homes in aesthetically pleasing ways.

Private Residence, Beverly Hills:

Graceful 12-foot (3.7-meter) Kentia Palms (*Howea Forsterana*) underplanted with Algerian Ivies (*Hedera canariensis*) and Dendrobium Orchids (*Dendrobium* spp.) are in the corners, while bowls of Phalaenopsis Orchids (*Phalaenopsis* spp.) repeat the gold-and-white color scheme that picks up the floral motif of the carpeting.

Yorkshire Residence
BEVERLY HILLS, CALIFORNIA

This small atrium in the entry of a large Beverly Hills home was a source of irritation for many years. Various interior landscape companies—and the owners themselves—had tried unsuccessfully to plant the atrium.

The interior landscape contractor who finally succeeded determined that the main problem was drainage, and decided to remove the existing soil and install a Mona-link system along with a light capillary mix. It was discovered, however, that only 12 inches (31 centimeters) down was a shale formation that created further drainage problems and restricted the root area. The shale was jack-hammered out to a depth that would accommodate the plants' root balls and allow them to drain.

Common Bamboos (*Bambusa vulgaris*) up to 16 feet (4.9 meters) were planted, tying into the existing design. The 45-gallon (171-liter) Bamboos were set over two connected 24-liter (6.3-gallon) Mona links. Cycads (*Dioon* sp.), (*Zamia furfuracea*), and (*Cycas circinalis*) were placed over a series of 7-liter (1.8-gallon) Mona links, with under-plantings of Black Cardinal Philodendron (*Philodendron*

1.

2.

3.

1. Looking down from the second floor, the foliage of the Bamboo *(Bambusa vulgaris)* seems to jump out of the adjacent wall covering.

2. An ordinary staircase is transformed into a vibrant focal point by this planter in the entrance of a Beverly Hills home.

3. The use of various Bromeliads, Cycads *(Cycas and Dioon* spp.*)*, and Zamias *(Zamia furfuracea)* achieve a tropical, colorful, and delightful impression for each visitor. Varying heights, variegated foliage, and careful placement keep the display interesting.

'Black Cardinal') and Silver Queen Chinese Evergreen *(Aglaonema 'Silver Queen')* around the base. A small Lady Palm *(Rhapis excelsa)* with a Bromeliad focal point at the foot of these stairs really accentuates this planter.

Private Residence

HIDDEN HILLS, CALIFORNIA

The interiorscape of this 22,000 square-foot (2,043.8 square-meter) residence in Hidden Hills, built in Mediterranean Style with a Santa Barbara interior, houses over 120 plants. The living room is close to 3,500 square feet (325.2 square meters), with a 25-foot (7.6-meter) ceiling and a built-in planter with Wine Palm *(Caryota urens)* and Fishtail Palm *(Caryota mitis)* in baskets around the perimeter, along with a large Peace Lily *(Spathiphyllum spp.)*. Furnishings are oversized to make the room seem less expansive.

A Mona sub-irrigation system reduces potential salt burn. Large specimen Bromeliads are underplanted with Black Cardinal Philodendron *(Philodendron 'Black Cardinal')*, Calatheas, and Jade Pothos *(Epipremnum aurem 'Tropic Green')*. Specimen Bromeliads are used throughout, with large Orchid *(Cymbidium spp.)* tubs at either side of the front door.

Hawaiian Ti Plant *(Cordyline terminalis)* is used in the kitchen area, and a Madagascar Dragon *(Dracaena marginata)* stump in a planter outside the master bedroom. The client did not want air conditioning to run in the guest wing

1.

2.

3.

except when occupied; the wing is thus planted with heat-tolerant large specimen 10-foot (3-meter) Euphorbia ingens, 9-foot (2.7-meter) Pencil Cactus, and a 9-foot (2.7-meter) Aloe bainesii.

4.

1. A close vertical view of the planter shows the restraint and simplicity that successfully draw attention to the room's sunwashed vaulted ceilings and travertine floors. Base plants include Xanthasoma, Philo, 'Black Cardinals', and 6-foot (1.8-meter) and 8-foot (2.4-meter) specimen Bromeliads.

2. Fishtail Palm *(Caryota mitis)*, Mauna Loa Peace Lily *(Spathiphyllum 'Mauna Loa')*, and table arrangements of Orchids *(Phalaenopsis and Cymbidium* spp.), Snake Plant *(Sansevieria* spp.), and Vriesea *(Vriesea capitilaere)* accentuate the warm natural environment.

3. An overview of the main room reveals the importance in placement and selection of the plant material. The sunny room, with its emphasis on natural wood and texture, required the casual elegance carvotas provide.

4. Eight Fishtail Palm *(Caryota mitis)* 14-foot (4.3-meter) specimens were used to complement the Wine Palm *(Caryota urens)* planter in the 3,500-square-foot (325-square-meter) living room, in addition to many plant arrangements in designer baskets and containers.

Private Residence
BEVERLY HILLS, CALIFORNIA

This 24,000-square-foot (2,230-square-meter) home in Beverly Hills uses widely divergent design motifs from one room to the next. The styles range from classical French in the living and dining rooms to transitional in the family room, to California contemporary in the loggia, and stark modern in the kitchen. With these many differing styles, foliage and flowering plants were among the elements used to tie the variations together. The design changes from formal to relaxed as public rooms transition into more private areas. In hallways and entries, arrangements face mirrors to create an illusion of a much larger arrangement and add dimension to the generally bare walls. The arrangements become living, changing art pieces. Orchids are used as a principal horticultural element, repeating one family of plants from room to room while allowing the varied colors of the blooms to blend with the decor of each. The average first-floor ceiling is 12 feet (3.7 meters) high, so large specimens are used throughout. More than one hundred Orchids, thirty-six Bromeliads, small foliage, and floor plants—319 specimens in all—have been installed.

1.

2.

3.

4.

1. The repeated theme of Kentia Palms *(Howea Forsterana)* used in the corners of the room helps unify the disparate interior design styles of the other rooms.

2. The living room has three 12-foot (3.7 meter) Kentia Palms *(Howea Forsterana)* underplanted with Algerian Ivies *(Hedera canariensis)* and Dendrobium Orchids *(Dendrobium* sp.*)*. Eight Oncidium Orchids *(Oncidium* sp.*)* were packed into the coffee table arrangement to achieve the desired look.

3., 4. Small potted Orchids placed in front of a mirror were intended to create the illusion of much larger arrangements and add dimensionality to the flat wall.

Matt Bird, Diversifolia, Inc.
St. Louis, Missouri

Private Residence
ST. LOUIS, MISSOURI

One of the more notable aspects of this small interior garden is the lack of a specimen with any real height to establish itself as a primary focal point in the space. Surprisingly, cost was not the driving force behind the use of only smaller plants. The garden situated in a part of the home where most of the sight lines through the garden and beyond can pick up a magnificent view of the exterior of the property, and it was mutually decided that the interior garden should not compete with the striking natural beauty of the adjacent forest setting.

The fountain brings the relaxing sound of trickling water, which adds to the relaxing ambiance created by the garden itself. By including a regular replacement program of potted flowering plants, the owners are able to change with the seasons or have a fresh look when they are entertaining. The overall effect is a perfect complement to the rich residential setting.

1.

1. The owner requested that the view to the surrounding exterior property not be blocked by tall foliage. The height was limited to one 7-foot (2.1-meter) Lady Palm *(Rhapis excelsa)*.

2. From the billiard room, the viewer sees an interesting variety of plant material.

3. Looking past the low fountain, one can see the deck just outside the house.

2.

3.

Nelson R. Hammer, Hammer Design
Boston, Massachusetts

The Landmark
BRAINTREE, MASSACHUSETTS

The former Central Junior High School in Braintree, Massachusetts was the subject of an unusual adaptive reuse into apartments in 1989. The classrooms around the periphery of the structure became living units, while the gymnasium and auditorium located in the core of the structure were removed to create a multi-story, skylit atrium filled with plants, water features, seating, and other amenities created to serve the residents of the building. Changes in elevation, created with concrete block walls and bluestone stairs help articulate the space at the floor level. The many features of the atrium can be observed from walkways on all three levels of the building.

1.

3.

2.

1. Dense ground covers and low-growing shrubs fill the planter beds near taller plantings of two Weeping Fig trees *(Ficus benjamina).*

2. Framed by the arch of the nearby colonnade, a Lance Dracaena *(Dracaena reflexa)* in the foreground and a multi-stemmed Weeping Fig tree *(Ficus benjamina)* are featured elements.

3. The key plant in this small planter is a Lance Dracaena *(Dracaena reflexa)*, underplanted with Jade Pothos *(Epipremnum aureum 'Tropic Green').*

Steve McCurdy, Landscape Images
Lake Forest, California

Muir Residence

SAN DIEGO, CALIFORNIA

This nearly 4,000-square-foot (360-square-meter) high-end residence was a challenge to the interior landscape designer/contractor from the start, because three different clients had to be satisfied: the home builder, who expected 50,000 people to see the residence over a period of six weeks, the house designer, who wanted the interior landscape to highlight the design, and the family that purchased the home and said they would buy the plantings if they like what was done.

1.

1. One of the home's three marble fireplaces forms the divider between the dining room and living room, while a 20-gallon (76-liter) Fishtail Palm *(Caryota mitis)* frames one side of the patio doors.

2. An Ali Fig Tree *(Ficus 'Alii')* stands in the corner, underplanted with Grape Ivy *(Cissus rhombifolia)*, while an Orchid *(Phalaenopsis sp.)* sits in a dish garden on the left.

[opposite] The Lady Palm *(Rhapis excelsa)* and floral arrangement provide a textural contrast to the rich buff tones of the family room's interior design.

2.

Hall Residence

KANSAS CITY, MISSOURI

The most interesting part of this project from an interior landscape standpoint is the indoor swimming pool. Two Pygmy Date Palms *(Phoenix roebelenii)* are placed symmetrically at the end of the room while the walls and ceiling have been planted with Creeping Fig *(Ficus pumila)*, which quickly took over.

1.

2.

3.

1. The children's pool has concentric rings with a bronze sitting fountain sprinkled in gold tiles depicting the constellations Orion, Pleiades, Ursa Minor and Major, and others.

2. Two Pygmy Date Palm *(Phoenix roebelenii)* underplanted with Boston Fern (Nephrolepis exaltata 'Bostoniensis') are placed symmetrically at the end of the room while the walls and ceiling have been planted with Creeping Fig *(Ficus pumila)*.

3. Interior swimming pool court, with rich materials and tropical plants.

Steve McCurdy, Landscape Images
Lake Forest, California

Private Residence

CORONA DEL MAR, CALIFORNIA

This residence is located in Pelican Point, a prestigious gated enclave in Corona del Mar, California. The marble floors and neutral color scheme of the home's entry and other areas relied heavily on interior plants to transform a relatively stark atmosphere into an inviting residential environment. Palms were used throughout to provide graceful, arching vertical elements, and were augmented by a substantial program of both permanent understory plantings and changing floral displays.

There are approximately 120 foliage and floral plants in the home, ranging in size from 4-inch (10.2 centimeter) potted table plants to 15-gallon (56.8-liter) floor plants. In addition to the live plantings, there are nineteen preserved topiaries in the home, ranging from 20 inches (50.8 centimeters) to 5 feet (1.5 meters) in height.

1.

2.

3.

1., 2. As one can well imagine, the room changes dramatically by the addition of foliage and florals, underscoring the importance of interiorscaping in creating vitality and warmth for human environments. The plants add textural richness to the hard flat lines of the architecture.

3. Underplantings of Starlite Peace Lily *(Spathiphyllum 'Starlite')*, Silver Queen Chinese Evergreen *(Aglaonema 'Silver Queen')*, Sensation Peace Lily *(Spathiphyllum 'Sensation')* in the rear. Green Jade Pothos *(Epipremnum aureum 'Tropic Green')*, and various Bromeliads throughout draw the eye downward and provide a functional expanse of color that absorbs sound (avoiding a museum-like atmosphere), freshens the air, and gives depth to the entry, creating an inviting rather than intimidating first impression.

Special

Collections of plants and animals in conservatories and zoos play an important role in revealing the secrets of nature for all ages, at a time when interest in conservation and biodiversity is at a new peak. Interior landscape designers and contractors employing the latest technologies are able to re-create virtually any exterior environment indoors and provide settings that enhance visitors' understanding of the plants and animals' relation to their habitat.

Replicating the outdoor environment indoors is no easy task. It can involve a deep understanding of natural ecosystems, and the selection and acclimatization of plant species often not previously used. Sophisticated environmental controls allow the design of ecosystems with the required air and soil temperatures, air circulation, and humidity. Supplementary lighting can adjust natural light levels. The result is an artificial habitat in which wildlife seems at home and unaffected by the stream of visitors.

Indoor facilities at Longwood Gardens in Kennett Square, Pennsylvania; at the New York Botanical Garden, Bronx, New York; and the Missouri Botanical Garden in St. Louis embody all that is best in conservatories across the U.S. and throughout the world. Conservatories provide ideal conditions for displaying a diverse range of species by maximizing light and optimizing moisture and humidity. Short-term fall and spring exhibits are possible even when outside conditions are unfavorable. As permanence is not a restriction and the plant palette is not confined to the hardiest species, a wide diversity may be exhibited throughout the year.

Regenstein Small Mammal and Reptile House, Lincoln Park Zoo

[opposite] A view from the upper level looking past the Australian Savanna toward the African exhibit.

McRae Anderson, McCaren Designs, Inc.
St. Paul, Minnesota

Tropical American Rain Forest Exhibit

TULSA ZOO AND LIVING MUSEUM, TULSA, OKLAHOMA

The exhibit is designed to be an immersion experience, giving the visitor a glimpse of the beauty and biodiversity of an actual rain forest. Over 250 different species of plants are represented within a 13,000-square-foot (1,208-square-meter) area. The various plant material—all of it native to Central and South America—was hand-selected for the exhibit. Due to the complexity of the construction, the project was completed in three phases over a seven-month period. The actual installation was preceded, however, by a year and a half of locating and purchasing the collection of rare and unusual plants. Since the primary focus was to exhibit plant species originating in the American tropics, zoo authorities insisted that all plant material be indigenous to Central or South America. Much time and research went into validating the origin of items on the master plant list. Many of the plants were collected from seeds and small cuttings, and then grown to maturity.

1.

2.

3.

4.

1. Sophisticated environmental controls installed in the building simulate natural conditions, promoting abundant growth and flowering. This Passion Vine *(Passiflora edulis)* was chosen for its prolific blooming habit.

2. Bordering the Mayan ruins are plants representing the agricultural richness of the tropical rain forest: Bananas *(Musa nana)*, Chocolate *(Theobroma cacao)*, Guava *(Psidium guava)*, and Tapioca *(Manihot esculenta)* are but a few of the plants represented in this collection.

3. Living plants blend with painted murals to create an illusion of depth within the animal enclosure. This habitat in the Flooded Forest contains the Caiman, a small alligator-like reptile.

4. Once construction was complete, plants and exhibit structures were seamlessly blended. Visitors are greeted by an Aztec bench sculpture. The artifact appears to be a remnant of a past civilization in the midst of an ecosystem that has returned to its natural state of dominance.

1.

2.

3.

4.

5.

1. Great care was taken with the handling of the larger trees. In addition to the unique specimens, much of the large material had a variety of epiphytic Spanish Moss *(Tillandsia useneoides)* attached to their branches.

2. Precision teamwork was needed to use the heavy equipment in tight quarters. The crew inside this part of the exhibit could not be seen by the crane operator; instructions had to be relayed back and forth. About 30 tons (27,216 kilograms) of material was transported to this hummingbird enclosure.

3. The planting specifications called for three layers of media. On the surface was a two-foot layer of customized planting media. A 1.5-foot (0.5-meter) sand/soil layer separates the surface media from the sharp sand drainage base. A total of 250 tons (226,796 kilograms) of planting media were installed.

4. Once the planting medium was in place, the foliage trucks began to arrive from Florida. With limited access to the site, all plants had to be off-loaded in the parking lot and then moved into the exhibit.

5. Real plants and artificial facsimiles blend seamlessly within the rain forest.

Larson Associates
Tucson, Arizona

Climatron, Missouri Botanical Garden
ST. LOUIS, MISSOURI

The Climatron, the geodesic greenhouse at the Missouri Botanical Garden in St. Louis, underwent a two-year renovation that was completed in 1990, thirty years after it first opened. The old, yellowed Plexiglas™ panes were replaced with new, energy-efficient laminated glass, and the Climatron's interior was redesigned. Improvements were not solely cosmetic: the Climatron's focus has shifted to include an educational component. As visitors experience the beauty and diversity of tropical plants, they also learn why rain forests are so diverse, vital, and endangered.

The interior re-creates a lush rain forest with waterfall, tropical plants, and aquatic life. From an elevated walkway visitors view epiphytic plants (Orchids, Bromeliads, and Ferns) that grow without soil, perched high in treetops.

Exhibits like the Fallen Log describe the role of decomposition and nutrient recycling. The "Talking Orchid" exhibit, a mechanical Orchid, teaches about the Orchid family—the world's largest family of flowering plants.

1.

The Climatron—the first geodesic dome used as a greenhouse—is 70 feet (21.3 meters) high, 175 feet (53.4 meters) in diameter, and covers 23,000 square feet (2,136.7 square meters). It follows structural principles established by the late R. Buckminster Fuller.

2.

1. Tropical trees, palms, and bamboos flourish in the original Climatron. All but the largest trees were removed during the renovation and reconstruction of the refurbished Climatron.

2. View of the tropical geodesic dome entrance, with the Milles Sculpture Garden in the foreground. The two sides are flanked by Bald Cypress trees (*Taxodium distichum*) and seven bronzes by Carl Milles highlighting the reflecting pools filled with water lilies.

3. Under the race of the Cascade Waterfall, visitors can imagine being under a tropical waterfall with the roots of tropical vines dangling all around.

3.

1.

2.

1. Newly fabricated concrete rocks, water feature, and tree-like epiphyte armature during construction. Some plants have been installed here.

2. Visitors can walk under the Cascade Waterfall, one of the main architectural features of the Climatron. Bromeliads crowd the rock face overhead, while pink Bougainvillea (*Bougainvillea* spp.) and rose Rondeletia (*Rondeletia* sp.) bloom along the walk.

3. An early-morning shower mimics a tropical thunderstorm washing clean the leaves of palms, Heliconias (*Heliconia* spp.), and tropical swamp plants.

3.

1.

2.

1. Trailing Passion Vines *(Passiflora spp.)* hang next to the Great Waterfall in the lower level of the Climatron, with a bamboo, teak, and steel bridge in the background.

2. Two species of Passion Flower vines are used on a wood trellis to screen the visitors' walkway.

3. A young Talipot Palm *(Corypha umbraculifera)* expands over the rustic-looking fiberglass visitor's bench.

4. A small forest waterfall greets visitors at the main entrance, with eight different kinds of palms surrounding the area.

3.

4.

CLR Design, Inc.
Philadelphia, Pennsylvania

Regenstein Small Mammal and Reptile House

LINCOLN PARK ZOO, CHICAGO, ILLINOIS

The Regenstein Small Mammal and Reptile House, a new building at Chicago's Lincoln Park Zoo, was designed to house animals in eight authentic ecosystems representing different parts of the world. Native plants were selected for each of the eight ecosystems. Extremely dense plantings had to be installed at acute angles to create the realistic wild look specified by the architect. A 30-foot (9.1-meter) tall artificial Strangler Fig features heavily planted hollow limbs and dozens of Bromeliads adhered to its sides. The artificial granite planters were located at various levels above a central walkway designed for foot traffic, creating a major accessibility problem for installation of the plants, some of which were over 28 feet (8.5 meters) tall with 36 inches (91.4 centimeters) root balls. A shooting-boom forklift was used for some of the specimens, but lack of space limited its use—it fit through the only access door with less than an inch to spare! Installation had to be done as other trades worked at the same time. The scope of work included media installation, drainage in planters, and sand in dry exhibits. The completed project involved over 1,500 plants of seventy-five different species.

1.

2.

1. Birdnest Ferns grow from a log straddling a walkway running through the ecosystems. An African Tulip tree (*Spathodea campanulata*) can be seen in the foreground.)

2. [left] The design uses plants of diverse nature arranged on upper and lower levels.

[opposite] Moss-lined mesh pockets were attached to the sides of the replica Strangler Fig to hold Orchids and Bromeliads.

Enid A. Haupt Conservatory, New York Botanical Garden
BRONX, NEW YORK

The Enid A. Haupt Conservatory of the New York Botanical Garden is the greatest of the Victorian-era conservatories built in the United States. Designed by Lord and Burnham, the premier greenhouse designers of their day, the conservatory —inspired by the Palm House at the Royal Botanical Gardens at Kew, England— was constructed in two stages between 1899 and 1902. The central Palm House, with a dome 90 feet (27.4 meters) high and rotunda 100 feet (30.5 meters) in diameter, is the largest single component of the conservatory, though it is flanked by ten pavilions in two lateral wings. The total area under glass is nearly one acre (4,047 square meters). One result of a recent four year, $25 million renovation is that the Conservatory has changed from a taxonometric or geographic presentation to one with an emphasis on specific natural habitats. The Chrysanthemum Festival displayed on these pages is typical of thematic presentations made throughout the year, which keeps the pavilions constantly changing color.

1.

2.

3.

1., 2., 3. Here are three views of the conservatory prior to the renovation, during the annual Chrysanthemum Festival.

Longwood Gardens

KENNETT SQUARE, PENNSYLVANIA

Longwood Gardens, one of the premier horticultural display venues in the world, was first established as an arboretum in 1798 by Joshua and Samuel Peirce. The land and its arboretum was purchased by Pierre S. du Pont in 1906 to preserve the trees, and Mr. du Pont personally oversaw many of the improvements until the Gardens were turned over to a foundation he set up in 1946. While the exterior gardens enjoyed an international notoriety early in this century, Longwood Gardens is now equally well known for its indoor displays. The first of many such structures for showcasing plants was built in 1914, a small conservatory adjacent to the original Peirce farmhouse which was planned by Mr. Du Pont because Longwood was so dreary during the winter. This was followed by a huge conservatory completed in 1921. In addition to an Orangery and Exhibition Hall, later indoor display facilities included an Azalea House (1928), a Desert House (1957), greenhouses devoted to tropicals (1958), a

1.

2.

1. Three Thread Palms (Washingtonia robusta) rise behind a glorious blend of colorful and richly textured evergreen shrubs, flowers, ornamental grasses, and ground covers.

2. Water, a relatively common element of interior garden design, shares much of the ground plane area with manicured lawn, a most UNcommon element of the interior garden.

3. Flowers of unusual shapes, sizes, and textures are always in bloom in world class conservatories such as Longwood Gardens.

3.

Palm House (1966), and lastly, another major glass house, the East Conservatory, replaced the Azalea House when it opened in 1973. The diversity of species visible in these venues makes Longwood Gardens a magnet for the horticulture enthusiast, scholar, or weekend gardener all year long.

Steve McCurdy, Landscape Images
Lake Forest, California

California Mart

LOS ANGELES, CALIFORNIA

The California Mart is the West Coast's main fashion showroom. This huge complex of buildings covers multiple blocks but was getting rather old and tired-looking. Built in the 1960s, it's only had minor cosmetic changes, until a new fashion center was proposed by another developer. To ensure tenant retention, major renovations were made to what was once an outside courtyard to change it into the current atrium central lobby.

The architects asked for a design consultation eighteen months before the installation. Plans were for twelve 25-foot (7.6-meter) Alexander Palm (*Ptychosperma elegans*) with base plantings in 4-foot (1.2-meter) square planters on casters (which was later reduced to six, due to budget). Three months before the expected completion, the proposal was accepted. The installation was not the easiest, as the marble floor was still being laid and many of the subcontracters were still drywalling and painting in the mad rush to the grand-opening deadline!

1.

2.

3.

1. The perfectly symmetrical 25-foot (7.6-meter) palms alleviate the vast scale and remoteness of the over 35-foot (10.7-meter) atrium ceiling, which would otherwise overwhelm buyers walking through the lobby. The resulting interiorscape provides a striking presentation.

2. The palm trees are evenly divided on either side of the atrium's expansion joint, which runs through the center of the atrium. The planters, each of which weighs approximately 1,500 pounds (675 kilograms), are regularly moved for parties or major show events, but they cannot cross this joint, or the marble will crack.

3. This atrium lobby is surrounded on all four sides by thirteen stories of showrooms and offices. Grow lights on a timer or photo electric cell were installed to supplement the daylight when the sun does not clear the building during the winter.

Stamford Town Center Fall and Spring Projects
STAMFORD, CONNECTICUT

The manager of the Stamford Town Center, a 1-million square-foot (90,000 square-meter) regional mall in southern Connecticut, wanted to recreate the colors and feelings of a New England fall season throughout their facility. The Center Court of the mall consists of four large planters that normally have foliage plants. These plants were removed and replaced with materials intended to create a fall festival.

Red sugar maples, 12 feet (3.7 meters) to 14 feet (4.3 meters) high, with yellow and orange leaves, surrounded by over two hundred live ornamental grasses set the stage for the display. Fifteen different varieties of Miscanthus and Pennisetum—two genera of ornamental grasses—were selected in heights ranging from 2 feet (.6 meters) to 5 feet (1.5 meters). Colors of the plumes ranged from soft reds, pastel pinks and natural whites to bold tans. All grasses had to be watered once a week in order to keep these natural fall foliage colors.

A great challenge was not only to supply hundreds of flowering bulbs or perennials in specific colors, but also to coordinate production of the flowering materials and branches for the twenty-two day show. Precise colors and combinations were extremely important and there was little room for error.

1.

3.

2.

1. Van Gogh's softer accents were created with blue Lark-spur *(Delphinium* spp.*)*; Grape Hyacinth *(Muscari* spp.*)*; pink Foxglove *(Digitalis* spp.*)*; purple, white, and pink Freesia *(Freesia* spp.*)* interspersed with green Lilyturf *(Liriope* spp.*)* and five types of living mosses.

2. Close-up of the rice lady on table with a cup and saucer. The Foxtail Grass *(Calamagrostis Arundinacea)* in the front works well with the blue Plumbago *(Plumbago* sp.*)* and yellow Daylilies *(Hemerocallis* spp.*)*.

3. Hundreds of red-range Tulips *(Tulipa* spp.*)*, blueGrape Hyacinth *(Muscari* spp.*)*, yellow Daffodils *(Narcissus* spp.*)*, Calla Lilies *(Zantedeschia aethiopica)*, crimson Ranunculus *(Ranunculus* spp.*)*, white Hydrangea *(Hydrangea* spp.*)* and cinnamon-colored Pansies *(Viola* spp.*)* were used.

Notes

Several explanatory notes may be helpful to readers of Interior Landscapes:

The taxonomy of interior plants can be problematic to the serious student of horticultural nomenclature. While interior plants have common names and botanical names like their exterior counterparts, it appears that standardization of plant names is much more prevalent with regard to exterior plants than interior plants. Interior plant common names vary drastically from region to region, which is understandable, but botanical names, which should in theory be standardized in Latin throughout the world, can be disturbingly diverse from one foliage nursery to another. Interior Landscapes attempts to provide a semblance of standardization to interior plant nomenclature by using Hortus Third (First Edition, 1976) as a primary source for plant names and spellings. However, one of the most important reasons for the dynamic growth of interior landscaping in recent years- the introduction of new species of plants that are more tolerant of interior landscape environmental conditions- has yielded a bewildering array of plant names that often are in conflict with traditional taxonomic practice. In cases where plant species have been introduced subsequent to the publishing of Hortus Third, we have yielded to common usage in the industry for both common and botanical names.

As a book focusing on the design of interior landscapes, we have given primary credit for each project displayed to the "interior landscape designer". This term, rather than "landscape architect", is used because many of the projects incorporated into the book were conceived and constructed as part of design-build contracts, in which the projects were designed by staff members (or owners) of interior landscape contracting firms with little or no academic training in landscape architecture. In addition, several interior landscapes were designed by the architects of the buildings themselves. There are also instances in which representatives of the owner's staff were comprehensively involved in the interior landscape design. We felt the term "interior landscape designer" was appropriate to cover this variety of backgrounds for people practicing this discipline. Those of you involved in the design and contracting professions will no doubt realize that in truth, the conceptual or final planning of many projects will be a collaboration between all the disciplines, even though one firm may receive the credit. Unless specifically known to the author, the role of interior landscape designer for each project was credited to the person(s) or firm(s) supplied by the sources of information and photography for each of the submitted projects.

Project Credits

SECTION ONE: COMMERCIAL

PARKWAY NORTH CENTER
Deerfield, Illinois

OWNER
CarrAmerica

ARCHITECT
Hammond, Beeby and Babka

INTERIOR LANDSCAPE DESIGNER
Johnson, Johnson, and Roy
303 North Main Street
Ann Arbor, MI 48104
313-662-4457

INTERIOR LANDSCAPE CONTRACTOR
Rentokil Environmental Services

PHOTOGRAPHER
Robert Specht, Rentokil Environmental
Services

744 OFFICE PARKWAY OFFICE BUILDING
St. Louis, Missouri

OWNER
Country Life Insurance

ARCHITECT
Robert Boland

INTERIOR LANDSCAPE DESIGNER
Matt A. Bird. A.A.S., C.L.P.
Diversifolia, Inc.
1227-31 Hanley Industrial Court
St. Louis, MO 63144
314-962-9430

INTERIOR LANDSCAPE CONTRACTOR
Diversifolia, Inc.

PHOTOGRAPHER
Marty Keeven, Keeven Photography

MENLO PARK MALL
Menlo Park, New Jersey

OWNER
Simon DeBartolo

INTERIOR LANDSCAPE DESIGNER
John Mini Indoor Landscapes
233 Fordham Street
City Island, NY 10464
718-885-2426

INTERIOR LANDSCAPE CONTRACTOR
John Mini Indoor Landscapes

PHOTOGRAPHER
John Mini Indoor Landscapes

MAYFAIR MALL
Wauwatosa, Wisconsin

OWNER
Froedtert – Mayfair, Inc.

ARCHITECT
Kober/Belluschi Associates

INTERIOR LANDSCAPE DESIGNER
Joe Karr & Associates
10 West Hubbard Street
Chicago, Illinois 60610
312-467-7059

INTERIOR LANDSCAPE CONTRACTOR
Maxine Interior Plantscape, Inc.

PHOTOGRAPHER
Joe Karr, Joe Karr & Associates

28 QUEEN'S ROAD CENTRAL BUILDING
Hong Kong, People's Republic of China

OWNER
Central Management

INTERIOR LANDSCAPE DESIGNER
M. Paul Friedberg & Partners
41 East 11th Street
New York, NY 10003
212-477-6366

INTERIOR LANDSCAPE CONTRACTOR
Parker Interior Plantscapes

PHOTOGRAPHER
Richard Parker, Parker Interior Plantscapes

COPLEY PLACE
Boston, Massachusetts

OWNER
JMB Urban

ARCHITECT
The Architects Collaborative, Inc.

INTERIOR LANDSCAPE DESIGNER
Nelson Hammer
The Architects Collaborative, Inc.
(now defunct)
now practicing as Hammer Design
286 Congress Street 6th floor

Boston, MA 02210-1038

617-338-8598

INTERIOR LANDSCAPE CONTRACTOR
Rentokil Environmental Services

PHOTOGRAPHERS
Nelson Hammer
Steve Rosenthal
Rendering by Howard Associates

LENOX SQUARE EXPANSION AND RENOVATION

Atlanta, Georgia

OWNER
Corporate Property Investors

ARCHITECT
RTKL Associates

INTERIOR LANDSCAPE DESIGNER
Lois S. Harrison, ASLA
Grover & Harrison, P.C.
605 37th Street South
Birmingham, AL 35222
205-322-6363

INTERIOR LANDSCAPE CONTRACTOR
Rentokil Environmental Services

PHOTOGRAPHER
John Grover

MAINE MALL RENOVATION

South Portland, Maine

OWNER
S. R. Weiner & Associates

ARCHITECT
ADD Inc.

INTERIOR LANDSCAPE DESIGNER
Nelson Hammer
Hammer Design
286 Congress Street, 6th floor
Boston, MA 02210-1038
617-338-8598

INTERIOR LANDSCAPE CONTRACTOR
Rentokil Environmental Services

PHOTOGRAPHER
Peter Vanderwarker

CHEM COURT

New York, New York

OWNER
Chemical Bank

ARCHITECT
HLW International LLP

INTERIOR LANDSCAPE DESIGNER
HLW International LLP
115 Fifth Avenue
New York, NY 10003
212-353-4607

INTERIOR LANDSCAPE CONTRACTOR
John Mini Indoor Landscapes

PHOTOGRAPHERS
George Cserna
Claude Emile Furones
McGown Photographers

WINTERGARDEN, BATTERY PARK CITY

New York City, New York

OWNER
Olympia & York Properties

ARCHITECT
Cesar Pelli

INTERIOR LANDSCAPE DESIGNER
Paul Friedberg & Partners
41 East 11th Street
New York, NY 10003
212-477-6366

INTERIOR LANDSCAPE CONTRACTOR
Original Installation: Parker Interior Plantscape
Current Installation: John Mini Indoor Landscapes

PHOTOGRAPHERS
Whitney Cox
M. Paul Friedberg & Partners
Richard Parker, Parker Interior Plantscape

590 MADISON AVENUE

New York City, New York

OWNER
Edward Minskoff

ARCHITECT
Edward Larrabee Barnes

INTERIOR LANDSCAPE DESIGNER
Robert Zion, Zion and Breen

P.O. Box 34
Imlaystown, New Jersey 08526
609-259-9555

INTERIOR LANDSCAPE CONTRACTOR
John Mini Indoor Landscapes

PHOTOGRAPHERS
Gans /Furones
Nelson Hammer

RIVER OAKS MALL

Calumet City, Illinois

OWNER
Urban Retail Properties

ARCHITECT
James P. Ryan Associates

INTERIOR LANDSCAPE DESIGNER
Wehler-Peterson and Associates, Ltd.
4 East Wilson Street, Suite 200
Batavia, IL 60510
630-761-8450

INTERIOR LANDSCAPE CONTRACTOR
Rentokil Environmental Services Inc.

PHOTOGRAPHER
Denise Breitfuss, Rentokil Environmental Services Inc.

SECTION TWO: CORPORATE

DEERE & COMPANY

Moline, Illinois

OWNER
Deere & Company

ARCHITECT
Kevin Roche John Dinkeloo and Associates

INTERIOR LANDSCAPE DESIGNER
Sasaki Associates
64 Pleasant Street
Watertown, MA 02172
617-926-3300

INTERIOR LANDSCAPE CONTRACTOR
Rentokil Environmental Services

PHOTOGRAPHER
Deere & Company

MINE SAFETY APPLIANCES COMPANY
Pittsburgh, Pennsylvania

OWNER
Mine Safety Appliances Company

ARCHITECT
The Design Alliance

INTERIOR LANDSCAPE DESIGNER
Joseph Hajnas & Elizabeth R. Manuck
Joseph Hajnas Associates, Inc.
One Bigelow Square
Pittsburgh, PA 15219
412-281-1221

INTERIOR LANDSCAPE CONTRACTOR
Plantscape, Inc.

PHOTOGRAPHER
Mine Safety Appliances Company

INTERNATIONAL MINERAL & CHEMICAL CORPORATION
Northbrook, Illinois

OWNER
International Mineral and Chemical
Corporation

ARCHITECT
Graham, Anderson, Probst & White

INTERIOR LANDSCAPE DESIGNER
Joe Karr & Associates
10 West Hubbard Street
Chicago, IL 60610
312-467-7059

INTERIOR LANDSCAPE CONTRACTOR
Rentokil Environmental Services

PHOTOGRAPHER
Joe Karr, Joe Karr & Associates

BRADFORD EXCHANGE
Niles, Illinois

OWNER
The Bradford Exchange

ARCHITECT
Weese Seegers Hickey Weese

INTERIOR LANDSCAPE DESIGNER
Joe Karr & Associates
10 West Hubbard Street
Chicago, IL 60610
312-467-7059

INTERIOR LANDSCAPE CONTRACTOR
Ronald R. Damgaard and Associates, Inc.

PHOTOGRAPHER
Joe Karr, Joe Karr & Associates

ROWLAND INSTITUTE FOR SCIENCE
Cambridge, Massachusetts

OWNER
Rowland Institute for Science

ARCHITECT
The Stubbins Associates

INTERIOR LANDSCAPE DESIGNER
The Stubbins Associates
1033 Massachusetts Avenue
Cambridge, MA 02138
617-491-6450
Supplemental Design/Build Work:
Zen Associates
124 Boston Post Road
Sudbury, MA 01776
978-443-6222

INTERIOR LANDSCAPE CONTRACTOR
Original: The Greenery
Subsequent Reconstruction: Zen Associates

PHOTOGRAPHERS
Nelson Hammer
Ed Jacoby

HERCULES-BRANDYWINE
Wilmington, Delaware

OWNER
State of Delaware, City of Wilmington, and
Hercules, Inc.

ARCHITECT
Kohn Pederson Fox

INTERIOR LANDSCAPE DESIGNER
Sasaki Associates
64 Pleasant Street
Watertown, MA 02172
617-926-3300

INTERIOR LANDSCAPE CONTRACTOR
Parker Interior Plantscape

PHOTOGRAPHER
Alan Ward, Sasaki Associates

AMERITECH CENTER CORPORATE HEADQUARTERS
Hoffman Estates, Illinois

OWNER
The Ameritech Companies

ARCHITECT
Lohan Associates
INTERIOR DESIGNER
The Environments Group

INTERIOR LANDSCAPE DESIGNER
Joe Karr, Joe Karr & Associates
10 West Hubbard Street
Chicago, IL 60610
312-467-7059

INTERIOR LANDSCAPE CONTRACTOR
Rentokil Environmental Services

PHOTOGRAPHER
Denise Breitfuss, Rentokil Environmental
Services
Joe Karr, Joe Karr & Associates

ANHEUSER BUSCH HEADQUARTERS
St. Louis, Missouri

OWNER
Anheuser Busch Breweries

ARCHITECT
Peckham, Guyton, Albers and Viets, Inc.

INTERIOR LANDSCAPE DESIGNER
Matt A. Bird, A.A.S., C.L.P.
Diversifolia, Inc.
1227-31 Hanley Industrial Court
St. Louis, MO 63144
314-962-9430

INTERIOR LANDSCAPE CONTRACTOR
Diversifolia, Inc.

PHOTOGRAPHER
Marty Keeven, Keeven Photography

FORD FOUNDATION BUILDING
New York City, New York

OWNER
Ford Foundation

ARCHITECT
Kevin Roche John Dinkeloo & Associates

INTERIOR LANDSCAPE DESIGNER
Office of Dan Kiley

East Farm
Charlotte, VT 05445
802-425-2141

INTERIOR LANDSCAPE CONTRACTOR
Original: Everett Conklin & Companies
Current: John Mini Indoor Landscapes

PHOTOGRAPHERS
John Mini Indoor Landscapes
Ford Foundation
Nelson Hammer

CIGNA
Bloomfield, Connecticut

OWNER
CIGNA Corporation

ARCHITECT
The Architects Collaborative, Inc.
(now defunct)

INTERIOR LANDSCAPE DESIGNER
The Architects Collaborative, Inc.
(now defunct)
now practicing as Hammer Design
286 Congress Street 6th floor
Boston, MA 02210-1038
617-338-8598

INTERIOR LANDSCAPE CONTRACTOR
John Mini Indoor Landscapes

PHOTOGRAPHER
Nelson Hammer

NATIONAL FIRE PROTECTION ASSOCIATION HEADQUARTERS
Quincy, Massachusetts

OWNER
National Fire Protection Association

ARCHITECT
Ben Thompson & Associates

INTERIOR LANDSCAPE DESIGNER
Zen Associates
124 Boston Post Road
Sudbury, MA 01776
978-443-6222

INTERIOR LANDSCAPE CONTRACTOR
Zen Associates

PHOTOGRAPHERS
Nelson Hammer
Zen Associates

INSIGNIA COMMERCIAL GROUP
Bingham Farms, Michegan

OWNER
Insignia Commercial Group

ARCHITECT
Seymour Levine Architects Inc.

INTERIOR LANDSCAPE DESIGNER
Larry M. Pliska
Planterra Tropical Greenhouses Inc.
7315 Drake Road
West Bloomfield, MI 48322
248-661-1515

INTERIOR LANDSCAPE CONTRACTOR
Planterra Tropical Greenhouses Inc.

PHOTOGRAPHER
Scott Benjamin

LDM TECHNOLOGIES INC.
Auburn Hills, Michegan

OWNER
LDM Technologies Inc.

ARCHITECT
Campbell Manix, Inc.

INTERIOR LANDSCAPE DESIGNER
Carey Baker
3621 Chevron
Highland, MI 48356
248-887-3303

INTERIOR LANDSCAPE CONTRACTOR
Planterra Tropical Greenhouses, Inc.

PHOTOGRAPHER
Scott Benjamin

STERLING DIRECT
St. Louis, Missouri

OWNER
Sterling Direct

ARCHITECT
Henderson Group

INTERIOR LANDSCAPE DESIGNER
Matt A. Bird, A.A.S., C.L.P.
Diversifolia, Inc.
1227-31 Hanley Industrial Court
St. Louis, MO 63144
314-962-9430

INTERIOR LANDSCAPE CONTRACTOR
Diversifolia, Inc.

PHOTOGRAPHER
Marty Keeven

BROWN FORMAN FORESTER CENTER
Louisville, Kentucky

OWNER
Brown Forman Distillery Company

ARCHITECT
Harry Weese & Associates

INTERIOR LANDSCAPE DESIGNER
Joe Karr, Joe Karr & Associates
10 West Hubbard Street
Chicago, IL 60610
312-467-7059

INTERIOR LANDSCAPE CONTRACTORS
Rentokil Environmental Services
Anything Grows

PHOTOGRAPHER
Joe Karr, Joe Karr & Associates

TRANS AM
Oakbrook Terrace, Illinois

OWNER
Trans Am Corporation

ARCHITECT
Solomon Cordwell Buenz & Associates

INTERIOR LANDSCAPE DESIGNER
Joe Karr & Associates
10 West Hubbard Street
Chicago, IL 60610
312-467-7059

INTERIOR LANDSCAPE CONTRACTOR
D. R. Church Landscape Company

PHOTOGRAPHER
Joe Karr, Joe Karr & Associates

BECTON DICKINSON HEADQUARTERS
Franklin Lakes, New Jersey

OWNER
Becton Dickinson and Company

ARCHITECT
Kallman McKinnell & Wood

INTERIOR LANDSCAPE DESIGNER
Building I:
Michael Singer, Artist
P.O. Box. 682 Parsons Road
Wilmington, VT 05363-0682
Morgan Wheelock, Landscape Architects
362 Summer Street
Somerville, MA 02144-3132
617-776-9300
Michael McKinnell, Kallman McKinnell &
Wood
939 Boylston Street
Boston, MA 02115-3106
617-267-0808
Building II:
Morgan Wheelock, Landscape Architects
362 Summer Street
Somerville, MA 02144-3132
617-776-9300
Kallman McKinnell & Wood
939 Boylston Street
Boston, MA 02115-3106
617-267-0808

INTERIOR LANDSCAPE CONTRACTOR
Building I:
Gilbane Building Company
Building II:
Henderson Corporation
Parker Interior Plantscape

PHOTOGRAPHER
Steve Rosenthal

SECTION THREE: HOSPITALITY

HYATT REGENCY GREENWICH
Greenwich, Connecticut

OWNER
Hyatt Hotels Corporation

ARCHITECT
Kohn Pederson Fox

INTERIOR LANDSCAPE DESIGNER
The Berkshire Design Group
4 Allen Place
Northampton, MA 01060
413-582-7000

INTERIOR LANDSCAPE CONTRACTOR
Original Installation: Decora
Current Installation: Parker Interior Plantscape

PHOTOGRAPHER
Nelson Hammer

MARRIOTT'S ORLANDO WORLD CENTER
Orlando, Florida

OWNER
Marriott Hotels

ARCHITECT
RTKL Associates, Inc.

INTERIOR LANDSCAPE DESIGNER
Scott Rykiel, Stuart Oftel
(currently of Mahan Rykiel Associates, Inc.,
Baltimore, MD)
LDR International
Quarry Park Place, Suite 100
9175 Guilford Road
Columbia, MD 21046-2660
410-792-4360

PHOTOGRAPHER
Photos courtesy of RTKL Associates, Inc. and
Mahan Rykiel Associates

CROWN CENTER HOTEL
Kansas City, MO

OWNER
Westin Hotels Corporation

ARCHITECT
Harry Weese Associates

INTERIOR LANDSCAPE DESIGNER
Mr. Robert Shaheen
Landscape Associates
8013 Counts Massie Road
Little Rock, AR 72113
800-374-4459

INTERIOR LANDSCAPE CONTRACTOR
Everett Conklin Companies

PHOTOGRAPHERS
Hallmark Cards
Nelson Hammer

WINDHAM HOTEL
Itasca, Illinois

OWNER
Patriot American Hospitality

INTERIOR LANDSCAPE DESIGNER
Denise Breitfuss

Rentokil Environmental Services
3750 W. Deerfield Road
Riverwoods, IL 60015
847-634-4250

INTERIOR LANDSCAPE CONTRACTOR
Rentokil Environmental Services

PHOTOGRAPHER
Denise Breitfuss, Rentokil Environmental
Services

EMBASSY SUITES HOTEL
Parsippany, New Jersey

OWNER
Embassy Suites Hotels

ARCHITECT
Perkins Eastman, Architects

INTERIOR LANDSCAPE DESIGNER
Parker Interior Plantscape
1325 Terrill Road
Scotch Plains, NJ 07076
908-322-5552

INTERIOR LANDSCAPE CONTRACTOR
Parker Interior Plantscape

PHOTOGRAPHER
Richard Parker, Parker Interior Plantscape

EMBASSY SUITES HOTEL
Deerfield, Illinois

OWNER
Felcor Lodging and Trust

ARCHITECT
Solomon Cordwell Buenz & Associates, Inc.

INTERIOR LANDSCAPE DESIGNER
James Martin Associates
24380 North Highway 45
Vernon Hills, Il 60061
708-634-1660

INTERIOR LANDSCAPE CONTRACTOR
Rentokil Environmental Services

PHOTOGRAPHER
Robert Specht, Rentokil Environmental Services

EMBASSY SUITES HOTEL
La Jolla, California

OWNER
Embassy Suites Hotels

ARCHITECT
Buss Silvers & Associates

INTERIOR LANDSCAPE DESIGNER
Steve McCurdy
Landscape Images
20611 Cañada Road
Lake Forest, CA
714-454-0123

INTERIOR LANDSCAPE CONTRACTOR
Landscape Images

PHOTOGRAPHER
Paul A. Kiler

THE EMERALD SHAPERY CENTER/PAN PACIFIC HOTEL
San Diego, CA

OWNER
Pan Pacific Hotels

ARCHITECT
Alan Turner, C.W. Kim, AIA

INTERIOR LANDSCAPE DESIGNER
Robin Shifflet
Wimmer Yamada
526 5th Avenue
San Diego, CA 92101
619-232-4004

INTERIOR LANDSCAPE CONTRACTOR
Landscape Images

PHOTOGRAPHER
Paul A. Kiler

SECTION FOUR: INSTITUTIONAL

LONDON STANDARD CHARTERED BANK
London, England

OWNER
London Standard Chartered Bank

ARCHITECT
Fitzroy Robinson Partnership

INTERIOR LANDSCAPE DESIGNER
Office of Dan Kiley
East Farm
Charlotte, VT 05445
802-425-2141

INTERIOR LANDSCAPE CONTRACTOR
Rochford Landscape, Ltd.

PHOTOGRAPHER
Aaron Kiley

CLASS OF 1959 CHAPEL, HARVARD BUSINESS SCHOOL
Cambridge, Massachusetts

OWNER
Harvard University

ARCHITECT
Moshe Safdie and Associates

INTERIOR LANDSCAPE DESIGNER
Peter Hornbeck & Associates
3 Johnson Street
North Andover, MA 01845
978-682-6116

INTERIOR LANDSCAPE CONTRACTOR
Peter L. Hornbeck & Associates

PHOTOGRAPHERS
Michal Ronnen Safdie
Steve Rosenthal

STATE OF ILLINOIS REVENUE CENTER
Springfield, Illinois

OWNER
State of Illinois Department of Revenue

ARCHITECT
Ferry & Henderson and A. Epstein and Sons, Inc.

INTERIOR LANDSCAPE DESIGNER
Joe Karr & Associates
10 West Hubbard Street
Chicago, IL 60610
312-467-7059

INTERIOR LANDSCAPE CONTRACTOR
Exotica, LTD.

PHOTOGRAPHER
Joe Karr, Joe Karr & Associates

MEMORIAL HEALTH CARE BUILDING
Worcester, Massachusetts

OWNER
Memorial Health Care

ARCHITECT
Shepley Bulfinch Richardson & Abbott

INTERIOR LANDSCAPE DESIGNER
Nelson R. Hammer, ASLA
Hammer Design
286 Congress Street, 6th Floor
Boston, MA 02210-1038
617-338-8598

INTERIOR LANDSCAPE CONTRACTOR
Rentokil Environmental Services

PHOTOGRAPHER
Richard Mandelkorn

HOWARD HUGHES MEDICAL INSTITUTE
Chevy Chase, Maryland

OWNER
Howard Hughes Medical Institute

ARCHITECT
The Hillier Group

INTERIOR LANDSCAPE DESIGNER
Louise Schiller Associates
132 Mercer Street
Princeton, New Jersey
609-683-1011
LDR International
Quarry Park Place, Suite 100
9175 Guilford Road
Columbia, MD 21046-2660
410-792-4360

INTERIOR LANDSCAPE CONTRACTOR
Ruppert Landscape

PHOTOGRAPHERS
Jeff Goldberg
Mark Ross

BETH ISRAEL HOSPITAL
New York, New York

OWNER
Beth Israel Hospital

ARCHITECT
Mitchell Associates

INTERIOR LANDSCAPE DESIGNER
John Mini Indoor Landscapes
233 Fordham Street
City Island, NY 10464
718-885-2426

INTERIOR LANDSCAPE CONTRACTOR
John Mini Indoor Landscapes

PHOTOGRAPHER
Whitney Cox

PIERPONT MORGAN LIBRARY
New York, New York

OWNER
Pierpont Morgan Library

ARCHITECT
Voorsanger & Mills Associates

INTERIOR LANDSCAPE DESIGNER
Office of Dan Kiley
East Farm
Charlotte, VT 05445
802-425-2141

INTERIOR LANDSCAPE CONTRACTOR
John Mini Indoor Landscapes

PHOTOGRAPHER
Dan Kiley

SECTION FIVE: RESIDENTIAL

YORKSHIRE RESIDENCE
Beverly Hills, California

OWNER
Analee Yorkshire

INTERIOR DESIGNER
Ron Wilson Interior Designs

INTERIOR LANDSCAPE DESIGNER
Steve McCurdy
Landscape Images
20611 Cañada Road
Lake Forest, CA 92630
714-454-0123

INTERIOR LANDSCAPE CONTRACTOR
Landscape Image

PHOTOGRAPHER
Paul A. Kiler

PRIVATE RESIDENCE
Hidden Hills, California

ARCHITECT
Robert Van Roeak

INTERIOR DESIGNER
Ron Wilson Interior Designs

INTERIOR LANDSCAPE DESIGNER
Steve McCurdy
Landscape Images
20611 Cañada Road
Lake Forest, CA 92630
714-454-0123

INTERIOR LANDSCAPE CONTRACTOR
Landscape Images

PHOTOGRAPHER
Paul A. Kiler

PRIVATE RESIDENCE
Beverly Hills, California

INTERIOR DESIGNER
Michael McCullough, Michael Brian Interior
Designs

INTERIOR LANDSCAPE DESIGNER
Steve McCurdy
Landscape Images
20611 Cañada Road
Lake Forest, CA 92630
714-454-0123

INTERIOR LANDSCAPE CONTRACTOR
Landscape Images

PHOTOGRAPHER
Paul A. Kiler

PRIVATE RESIDENCE
St. Louis, Missouri

ARCHITECT
Chesterfield Homes

INTERIOR LANDSCAPE DESIGNER
Matt A. Bird. A.A.S., C.L.P.
Diversifolia, Inc.
1227-31 Hanley Industrial Court
St. Louis, MO 63144
314-962-9430

INTERIOR LANDSCAPE CONTRACTOR
Diversifolia, Inc.

PHOTOGRAPHER
Marty Keeven, Keeven Photography

THE LANDMARK
Braintree, Massachusetts

OWNER
F.X. Messina

ARCHITECT
Eden Milroy & Associates

INTERIOR LANDSCAPE DESIGNER
Nelson R. Hammer, ASLA
Hammer Design
286 Congress Street, 6th Floor
Boston, MA 02210-1038
617-338-8598

INTERIOR LANDSCAPE CONTRACTOR
Rentokil Environmental Services

PHOTOGRAPHER
Nelson Hammer

MUIR RESIDENCE
San Diego, California

ARCHITECT
Bowlus, Edinger & Starck

INTERIOR LANDSCAPE DESIGNER
Steve McCurdy
Landscape Images
20611 Cañada Road
Lake Forest, CA 92630
714-454-0123

INTERIOR LANDSCAPE CONTRACTOR
Landscape Images

PHOTOGRAPHER
Paul A. Kiler

HALL RESIDENCE
Kansas City, Missouri

OWNER
Donald & Adele Hall

ARCHITECT
Taft Architects

INTERIOR LANDSCAPE DESIGNER
Office of Dan Kiley
East Farm
Charlotte, VT 05445
802-425-2141

INTERIOR LANDSCAPE CONTRACTOR
Rosehill Gardens, Inc.

PHOTOGRAPHER
Aaron Kiley

PRIVATE RESIDENCE
Corona del Mar, California

INTERIOR DESIGNER
Michael McCollough, Michael Brian Interior
Designers

INTERIOR LANDSCAPE DESIGNER
Steve McCurdy
Landscape Images
20611 Cañada Road
Lake Forest, CA 92630
714-454-0123

INTERIOR LANDSCAPE CONTRACTOR
Landscape Images

PHOTOGRAPHER
Eric Figge

SECTION SIX: SPECIAL

**TROPICAL AMERICAN RAIN FOREST
EXHIBIT, TULSA ZOO AND LIVING
MUSEUM**
Tulsa, Oklahoma

OWNER
Tulsa Zoo and Living Museum

ARCHITECT
Fritz Bailey, Inc.

INTERIOR LANDSCAPE DESIGNER
McRae Anderson
McCaren Designs, Inc.
760 Vandalia Street, Suite 100
St. Paul, MN 55114
612-646-4764

EXHIBIT DESIGNER/ARTIFICIAL PLANT
FABRICATOR
The Larson Company

INTERIOR LANDSCAPE CONTRACTOR
Rentokil Environmental Services

PHOTOGRAPHER
Denise Breitfuss, Rentokil Environmental
Services

**CLIMATRON, MISSOURI BOTANICAL
GARDEN**
St. Louis, Missouri

OWNER
The Missouri Botanical Garden

ARCHITECT
Mackey, Mitcheal & Associates

INTERIOR LANDSCAPE DESIGNER/EXHIBIT
DESIGNER
Missouri Botanical Garden
4344 Shaw Blvd.
St. Louis, Missouri 63166-0299
314-577-5100
Larson Associates
Tucson, AZ

INTERIOR LANDSCAPE CONTRACTOR
MBG
Larson Associates (artificial foliage)
Hydro dramatic (waterfalls)

PHOTOGRAPHER
Jack Jennings, Missouri Botanical Garden

**REGENSTEIN SMALL MAMMAL AND
REPTILE HOUSE, LINCOLN PARK ZOO**
Chicago, Illlinois

OWNER
Lincoln Park Zoo

ARCHITECT
CLRdesign

INTERIOR LANDSCAPE DESIGNER
Jon Coe, CLRdesign
115 North 3rd Street
Phildelphia, Pennsylvania 19106
215-925-1002

INTERIOR LANDSCAPE CONTRACTOR
Rentokil Environmental Services

PHOTOGRAPHER
Aran Kessler

**ENID A. HAUPT CONSERVATORY, NEW
YORK BOTANICAL GARDEN**
Bronx, New York

OWNER
New York Botanical Garden

ARCHITECT
Original Design: Lord and Burnham
Restoration: Beyer Blinder Belle

INTERIOR LANDSCAPE DESIGNER
On-going displays:
New York Botanical Garden
200th Street and Southern Blvd.
The Bronx, NY
718-817-8700

Restoration:
Jon Coe, CLRdesign
115 North 3rd Street
Phildelphia, Pennsylvania 19106
215-925-1002

INTERIOR LANDSCAPE CONTRACTOR
New York Botanical Garden

PHOTOGRAPHER
Nelson Hammer

LONGWOOD GARDENS
Kennett Square, Pennsylvania

OWNER
Longwood Gardens

ARCHITECT
Richard Phillips Fox

INTERIOR LANDSCAPE DESIGNER
Longwood Gardens
Route 1, P. O. Box 501
Kennett Square, Pa 19348-0501
610-388-1000

INTERIOR LANDSCAPE CONTRACTOR
Longwood Gardens

PHOTOGRAPHER
L. Albee/Longwood Gardens

CALIFORNIA MART
Los Angeles, California

OWNER
California Mart

ARCHITECT
Robert Puleo, Langdon Wilson

INTERIOR LANDSCAPE DESIGNER
Steve McCurdy
Landscape Images
20611 Cañada Road
Lake Forest, California 92630
714-454-0123

INTERIOR LANDSCAPE CONTRACTOR
Landscape Images

PHOTOGRAPHER
Kiler Photography

**STAMFORD TOWN CENTER FALL AND
SPRING PROJECTS**
Stamford, Connecticut

OWNER
Stamford Town Center

INTERIOR LANDSCAPE DESIGNER
Howard K. Freilich
Blondie's Treehouse
21 North Avenue
Larchmont, NY 10538-2415
914-834-6300

INTERIOR LANDSCAPE CONTRACTOR
Blondie's Treehouse

PHOTOGRAPHER
Howard K. Freilich